Conspiracy Journal Presents:

STRANGE AND UNEXPLAINABLE DEATHS AT THE HANDS OF THE SECRET GOVERNMENT

By
Commander X & Tim R. Swartz

With Special Introduction By
Tim R. Swartz
Editor of Conspiracy Journal

GLOBAL COMMUNICATIONS

STRANGE AND UNEXPLAINED DEATHS AT THE HANDS OF THE SECRET GOVERNMENT

By Commander X & Tim R. Swartz

ISBN: 1892062879
Current Affairs

Timothy Green Beckley: Editorial Director
Carol Rodriguez: Publishers Assistant
Cover Art: Tim Swartz

For free catalog write:
Global Communications
P.O. Box 753
New Brunswick, NJ 08903

Free Subscription to Conspiracy Journal E-Mail Newsletter
www.conspiracyjournal.com

Contact Rights Manager at above address
For reprints and translations

CONTENTS

Introduction
By Tim Swartz, Editor *Conspiracy Journal*

It is always sad when someone dies unexpectedly. The shock and grief that comes with the loss of a loved one, for a while at least, can be almost too much to bear. Whether it is by accident or natural causes, death is a sad, yet certain, fact of life.

It is therefore terrible to contemplate a scenario where death comes not by natural causes, but at the hands of an assassin, sent with the sole purpose of murder. Not just any kind of murder. Not a murder of passion, or the accidental death from an anonymous robbery for the contents of a wallet or purse; but a secret murder. Homicide for the reason of silence, political or social justifications – murder to shut a mouth forever.

It seems more like a spy novel, or the plot to an action movie rather than real life. However, real life is often a lot more shocking than even the wildest stories cooked up by Hollywood writers. And the beauty of real life is that most secret murders are so successful that even the slightest questions are greeted with snorts of disgust and cries of "conspiracy nut."

After all, skeptics say that there are no conspiracies. The government, military, intelligence organizations, terrorists, secret groups, etc. don't conspire to murder people. They just die by accident or suicide, but not by any conspiracy. Now just tell that to the families of the victims of the terrorist attack of 9/11 – that there was no conspiracy – I'm sure that they would disagree.

So of course conspiracies exist. They happen everyday. To ignore and ridicule the facts just because they happen to have been lumped into a "conspiracy theory" is asinine and ignorant, and plays right into the hands of the conspirators.

For many, to deny that people have been murdered because of a conspiracy is a way to protect their own sanity. To keep safe their preconceived notions on what really goes on in the world around them. They refuse to believe that not only can such murders and assassinations happen in the first place, but that the murderers could also be victims themselves: victims of mind control to make them the perfect killing machine.

It is disturbing to think that strange, unexplainable deaths do take place. But who is ordering these deaths in the first place? Are several groups competing against each other; or does one powerful organization have an ultimate goal of world domination?

CHAPTER ONE
People Die Every Day

David Kelly was a British Ministry of Defence (MoD) weapons expert and scientific adviser to the proliferation and arms control secretariat for more than three years. He was an expert in arms control, working as a weapons inspector in Iraq between 1991 and 1998, following the first Gulf War.

Dr. Kelly became senior adviser on biological warfare for the UN in Iraq in 1994, holding the post until 1999. He was sufficiently well respected to have been nominated for a Nobel peace prize by the man who led the Iraq weapons inspections for much of the 1990s, Rolf Ekeus.

During a lecture Dr. Kelly once said: "When Iraq invaded Kuwait in August 1990, little did I realize that Saddam Hussein would dictate the next 10 years of my life."

He also led all the visits and inspections of Russian biological warfare facilities from 1991 to 1994 under the 1992 Trilateral Agreement between the U.S., UK and Russia. His friends knew him as a quiet man who did his job with the highest professional standards.

Part of his job was to brief journalists on defense issues. And he also had contact with MI6 director Sir Richard Dearlove and others within the Secret Intelligence Service. Perhaps it was his contacts with British journalists that lead to his problems and eventual suspicious death.

In 2003, the BBC reported that Downing Street had "sexed up" a September dossier on Iraq's alleged weapons of mass destruction against the wishes of the intelligence service. BBC defense correspondent Andrew Gilligan later accused the government's director of communications, Alastair Campbell, in a newspaper article of hyping intelligence to justify the war, in particular a line that Iraq had the capability of launching a chemical or biological attack within 45 minutes of an order being given.

Gilligan had quoted an unnamed senior British intelligence official as the source of the information. The source said the 45-minute claim was a "classic example" of how uncorroborated evidence was given undue prominence, especially as it allegedly came from only one source.

The Blair government fiercely denied the allegation in an increasingly bitter row between itself and the BBC. The government demanded to know the name of the source, accusing the BBC of poor journalistic practice. It said allegations that intelligence had been invented to back its case for war were "absurd."

Campbell threatened legal action against Gilligan, while the reporter countered with a threat to sue the government official. The BBC backed its reporter, including the board of governors who met hours before Gilligan was due to appear before the Foreign Affairs Select Committee – a panel of MPs investigating the government's claims about Iraq's weapons of mass destruction. They said the government was using the issue as a "smokescreen" to avoid the fact that no WMD had been found. In fact, the government never expected to find WMD in Iraq.

Strange and Unexplained Deaths at the Hands of the Secret Government

On July 9, 2003 the Ministry of Defence named David Kelly as a contact who it believed briefed Gilligan about Iraq's weapons program. Kelly admitted that he had met Gilligan a week before the story appeared on the BBC's Today program. However, Kelly denied that he was the main source for the story. He said that Gilligan's account of his conversation with his source was so different from their conversation he did not believe he could be the source.

Kelly was subjected to intense questioning from the media and a committee of politicians about his connections to the BBC story. On July 15 he appeared before a parliamentary inquiry and was accused of being a "fall guy." His disclosure prompted an angry reaction from MPs on the committee, who claimed he had been set up by the MoD.

Opposition Conservative MP Sir John Stanley said Kelly had acted in a "proper and honorable manner" in coming forward to suggest that he may have been Gilligan's source but had been "thrown to the wolves" by the MoD.

"You were being exploited to rubbish Mr. Gilligan and his source," he said. Labour MP Andrew Mackinlay said he believed Kelly was "chaff," thrown up by the MoD to divert attention.

"Have you ever felt like the fall guy? You have been set up, haven't you?" he told him. Kelly replied: "I accept the process."

On Thursday, July 17, sometime between 3:00 and 3:30PM, Dr.. David Kelly started out on his usual afternoon walk. About 18 hours later, searchers found his body, left wrist slit, in a secluded lane on Harrowdown Hill. There is more than adequate cause to question the current interpretation of the scientist's death, as set forth by the official report. The official version can be summarized as follows.

Between 3:00 and 3:20PM on July 17, 2003, Dr.. Kelly left his Oxfordshire residence after telling his wife he was going for his regular walk. At about 9:20AM on July 18, volunteer searchers in a wooded area on Harrowdown Hill found his body. On the body was a mobile telephone, glasses, key fob, and three 10-tablet blister packs of Coproxamol with one tablet remaining. Near the body was a Barbour cap, wristwatch, Sandvig knife, and half-liter bottle of water.

From this it was concluded that although he suffered from no significant mental illness, by the afternoon of July 17 Dr. Kelly was feeling isolated and hopeless. When he left the house he took with him several packets of his wife's prescription pain medication, a gardening knife from his desk drawer, and a bottle of water.

He proceeded to one of his favorite haunts, a peaceful and secluded spot, where sometime between 4:15PM and 1:15AM he removed his watch and glasses, swallowed over 20 pills, and repeatedly slashed at his left wrist, leaving the radial artery intact but completely severing the ulnar artery which caused him to bleed to death, most of the blood soaking into the detritus of the woodland floor.

In the process of stumbling or thrashing about in the undergrowth he possibly sustained minor abrasions to the scalp and lower lip, along with bruising to the lower legs and left side of chest. A less than fatal but more than therapeutic blood level of dextropropoxyphene, paracetamol, and clinically silent coronary artery disease had hastened his death.

SUICIDE OR MURDER

The official report, written by Judge Lord Hutton, concluded that Dr. Kelly had killed himself by cutting his left wrist after taking co-proxamol painkillers, adding that there was no evidence whatsoever that any third party had been involved.

However, two medics who examined Kelly's body were surprised that the official report ruled his death a suicide. Paramedic Vanessa Hunt and ambulance technician Dave Bartlett said they were struck by how little blood was seen on and around the body of David Kelly, which they thought was inconsistent with a fatal cut of an artery. They had raised the same concerns before but offered no alternative theory of the cause of death.

"We felt that our observations of the scene where Dr.. Kelly's body was discovered were inconsistent with the conclusion of the Hutton Inquiry that Dr.. Kelly's death resulted from the wound to his wrist," the pair said in a joint statement read by Bartlett at a news conference.

Hunt added: "When we arrived on the scene there was no gaping wound, there wasn't a puddle of blood around. There was a little bit of blood on the nettles to the left of his left arm. But there was no real blood on the body of the shirt. If you manage to cut a wrist and catch an artery you would get a spraying of blood, regardless of whether it's an accident. Because of the nature of an arterial cut, you get a pumping action. I would certainly expect a lot more blood on his clothing, on his shirt. If you choose to cut your wrists, you don't worry about getting blood on your clothes. I didn't see any blood on his right hand. If he used his right hand to cut his wrist, you would expect some spray," the paramedic said.

Ms Hunt's claims were backed by a number of prominent experts, including Dr. Bill McQuillan, a former consultant at Edinburgh's Royal Infirmary, who for 20 years has dealt with hundreds of wrist accidents.

"I have never seen one death resulting from cutting an ulnar artery," Dr. McQuillan said. "I can't see how he would lose more than a pint of blood by cutting the ulnar."

Other experts have expressed varying degrees of skepticism about whether Kelly could have died from cutting his wrist. A former M16 agent told a UK journalist that he had been taught how to "make anything look like anything" and said that evidence shows that there must have been some kind of struggle at the scene of Kelly's death.

The agent said it was sloppy work that Kelly's body was found with enough pills for an overdose but hadn't ingested them, he said that should have been removed from the scene under normal procedure. He added, "You can slit someone's wrists and make it look like suicide easily but it's a lot harder to make someone swallow tablets."

He also said the heart monitor pads found on Kelly's chest were "simply there to make sure he was dead." He also said those should have been removed and suspects the agents involved were disturbed by someone in the process of the killing.

Strange and Unexplained Deaths at the Hands of the Secret Government

Michael Shrimpton, a national security barrister in government matters, told radio host Alex Jones that Dr. Kelly had been murdered. Shrimpton said that within 48 hours of Kelly's death a British intelligence officer had contacted him and told him that Kelly had been murdered.

"That didn't take me by surprise," Shrimpton said. "I was suspicious of the suicide theory from the word go. Now that source told me he'd done some digging and discovered that it had been known in Whitehall that David Kelly was going to be taken down."

Shrimpton told Jones that in his opinion Dr. Kelly was probably murdered by an intravenous injection of Dextropropoxythene and paracetamol, the constituents of Co-Proxamol, and a muscle relaxant called Succinylcholine.

"Now Succinylcholine is a favorite method of assassinating people," Shrimpton said. "It's used by intelligence agencies, particularly the French DGSE. 30 milligrams of Succinylcholine, used in combination with the constituents of Co-Proxamol, would probably have been a lethal dose. The problem for someone investigating an assassination by Succinylcholine is that it metabolizes even after death and you only pick up the metabolites. In other words it's one of those drugs that leave's no trace unless you have a very expert pathologist who really knows what he or she is doing. It's fairly clear to me that the slash to the wrist was done to disguise the puncture wound. "

Shrimpton also said that his sources indicated that Dr. Kelly's death had been orchestrated by the French external intelligence agency the DGSE or Direction Générale de la Sécurité Extérieure.

"The indications are that the tasking for the assassination came from within the UK, went to Paris, was then OK'd in Paris, and on the information available to me, the operational agency for the assassination was DGSE. Now there are also indications that DGSE, in order to false-flag the assassination, should their team be discovered, used Iraqi intelligence assets from the Iraqi Mukhabarat agency that were available in Damascus after the fall of Baghdad."

"I have one source suggesting that an Iraqi team, that's to say an ex-Mukhabarat team, recruited in Damascus with the assistance of the Syrian intelligence operation, also the Mukhabarat, were flown into Corsica in the seven days prior to the assassination of David Kelly. Now the standard French practice when they carry out assassinations is to take their own team out. I am very doubtful that any of the people involved directly in the assassination of David Kelly are still alive. It's not likely that the French would let anyone survive."

According to Shrimpton, Kelly was murdered because he had been talking to the press and there was a fear of what else he might discuss with journalists. Furthermore, Kelly was due to return to Iraq and may have learned fresh information on that trip which Whitehall could not afford to trust him with.

Mai Pederson, a United States Air Force translator and close friend of Dr. Kelly, claimed that Kelly received death threats because of his work in Iraq. She said she was surprised that he had apparently taken 20 painkillers before slashing his wrist in remote woodland - because he had an aversion to swallowing tablets. In a statement to police she said Dr. Kelly had told her he would "never" commit suicide and that he feared he would be found "dead in the woods."

DEAD BEFORE THEIR TIME

It should come to no surprise that Dr. David Kelly's controversial death is just one of many that has occurred throughout history. Unfortunately, such deaths, by their very nature, often disappear under the radar of suspicion so that there is little way to calculate just how many people have died less-than-natural deaths.

Anyone in the public spotlight, royalty, movie stars, politicians, journalists, scientists, singers, who dies before their time is often suspected of being murdered by nefarious forces. President John F. Kennedy, his brother Robert Kennedy, John F. Kennedy Jr., Marilyn Monroe, Bruce Lee, his son Brandon Lee, John Lennon, Jayne Mansfield, Princess Diana, Jim Morrison, Former CIA Director William Colby, Danny Casolaro, Missouri Governor Mel Carnahan, Senator Paul Wellstone, Jim Keith, Ron Bonds – are just a few of the possibly thousands of suspicious deaths that have not gone unnoticed by the league of conspiracy researchers who are always seeking the connections that may evade the rest of us.

A good example was the untimely death of chemist Geetha Angara in February 2005. A chemist by trade, Angara had spent more than a decade around the massive Passaic Valley Water Commission storage tanks in Totowa, New Jersey, which she routinely tested for water quality. That experience has heightened the mystery of how the 43-year-old mother of three ended up dead at the bottom of a tank; her body was discovered after she had been missing for a day, authorities said.

Police divers had searched the dark and near-freezing waters of the tanks after PVWC officials reported Angara missing to Totowa police following her day shift. Angara was believed to have been taking water quality readings in the tanks when she was last seen.

Police have not ruled out any possible explanations for her death. Meanwhile, the family of the victim, a senior chemist at the plant for 12 years, questioned what could have gone wrong.

"We're investigating it as though it was a homicide," said Passaic County Prosecutor James Avigliano. "It's possible it was just an accident, but it's a very difficult situation to explain."

Among the unanswered questions was how Angara entered the tank, which is accessible by a hatch and normally covered, authorities said. Angara's body was found in a sump at the bottom of a 30-foot-deep tank, authorities said. With her body was a hand-held radio and clipboard.

Angara was last seen just before she set out to take water readings, authorities said. A co-worker found her cellphone and purse at her workstation hours after her 8:00AM to 4:00PM Tuesday shift had ended. Officials called Totowa police at 7:30 p.m. to report her missing.

Totowa Police Chief Robert Coyle, however, said he knew nothing about a 7:30PM call and that the first call his department received was at 11:22PM. Angara's sister questioned how the death could have occurred and why the disappearance was not noticed earlier among the plant's 80 workers. Authorities said there were no surveillance cameras in the area where Angara was testing water.

"I don't understand this," Saranya Rao said when she learned that her sister's body had been found. "I just don't know. Why didn't they know? Why didn't they miss her?"

Angara's family thought something was wrong after waiting hours for her to come home for dinner, Rao said. They tried calling Angara at work and on her cellphone, but received no answer.

The plant, which serves 800,000 North Jersey customers, was closed at 2:00PM Wednesday. Within hours, workers opened valves that released millions of gallons of treated water, emptying tanks to a level that allowed divers a clearer view of the bottom. Only after the tanks were completely empty did officers discover the body.

Angara's sister, Saranva Rao went to the plant late Tuesday, then returned to Angara's house at 3:00AM Wednesday. Soon after, authorities at the plant told Rao's husband, who also was at the plant, that he should go home for the night. He was given Angara's keys to her tan Nissan Maxima so that he could drive back to Holmdel, Rao said.

Prosecutor James Avigliano called it "unfortunate" that the car was driven away before investigators could examine it. It was later returned and authorities brought it to a crime scene lab in Haledon, Avigliano said.

"It might have been better had we been called in sooner," the prosecutor said.

Coyle said his officers looked at the car and did not find anything unusual about it before turning the keys over to Angara's brother-in-law. Avigliano questioned what he characterized as a lag in the missing persons report by Totowa police to county officials. Totowa police waited until about 11:00PM Tuesday to contact the Sheriff's Department's Special Crimes Unit, which then sent divers, Avigliano said.

Sheriff Jerry Speziale found out about the case about 8:00AM. Wednesday and notified the Prosecutor's Office, Avigliano said.

"It should not have happened like that, but it did," Avigliano said. "It's something that will be addressed."

The unusual circumstances surrounding the death of chemist Geetha Angara are strange to say the least. How she ended up on the bottom of a 30-foot-deep closed water tank is still a mystery. However, evidence does seem to point to murder by an unknown assailant or assailants.

In these days of terrorism, and fear of terrorism, a municipal water supply, like the massive Passaic Valley Water Commission that supplies water for the area around Totowa, New Jersey, could be the perfect location for some kind of terrorist operation to taint the water and poison thousands of unsuspecting people. Perhaps Angara, in her daily job as the chemist who kept tabs on the tanks water quality unwittingly stumbled across such a plot and paid the ultimate price for her knowledge. The question remains, who is it that might be interested in public drinking water along the east coast; foreign terrorists, or a secret, domestic group that wants to make it look like foreign terrorists are involved?

STRANGE CIRCUMSTANCES AROUND THE DEATH OF PRINCESS DIANA

The unexpected death of a beloved public figure creates a state of shock and profound loss within a large segment of the world's population. Such was the case when Diana the Princess of Wales died from injuries sustained during a car crash in Paris on August 31, 1997. Almost immediately evidence seemed to indicate that Diana's tragic death was not an accident and investigators like Brian Desborough, the late Jim Keith, and Brad Steiger uncovered facts that could reveal the true nature of Diana's premature death.

On August 30 1997, a Mercedes limo, escorted by a Range Rover, transported Diana and Dodi Al Fayed from Le Bourget airport to the Villa Windsor, which had been leased from the French government by Dodi's father, then drove to the Al Fayed owned Ritz Hotel. That evening, the couple was driven to Dodi's apartment, where they dressed for dinner, and returned to the Ritz. Dodi's personal chauffeur Philippe Dourneau, drove the limo on both trips.

On the latter trip, Dourneau took the shortest route between the Ritz and the apartment. In a purported effort to elude paparazzi, the couple left the hotel by a rear exit shortly after midnight in a Mercedes S280 limo, en route for Dodi's apartment. The vehicle was much lighter than the previous limo (a Mercedes 600) thus rendering it much more vulnerable than the earlier used limo in the event of a crash, and was driven by Henri Paul, the acting Head of Security at the Ritz. Why was Paul, who had left for the night, recalled to drive the vehicle instead of a professional chauffeur? Unlike Dourneau, Henri Paul wasn't licensed to drive either limo.

Instead of taking the shortest route to Dodi's apartment, Paul took a circuitous route in a direction away from the apartment. Three paparazzi later claimed that Paul departed the Ritz at a high speed. This claim was contradicted by footage from the hotel's security cameras showing the Mercedes leaving at a normal speed, with Paul driving in a responsible manner.

According to the police, Henri Paul's blood alcohol level was very high, yet the Ritz security cameras revealed that Paul arrived at the hotel shortly after 10:00PM and displayed no erratic behavior while parking his car, or later in the hotel. Upon arrival at the hotel, Paul was in regular contact with Al Fayed bodyguards Trevor Rees-Jones and "Kes" Wingfield. Neither of them observed any evidence suggesting that Henri Paul was intoxicated.

Investigative Judge Hervé Stephan attributed the crash to Henri Paul's drunkenness, yet failed to interview key witnesses such as bodyguard Trevor Rees-Jones or persons claiming to have observed a collision between the Mercedes and a white Fiat Uno.

Because of Diana's fear of assassination by security forces, the couple decided to place their safety solely in the hands of Al Fayed bodyguards and Dodi waved away the police escort. This was a fatal mistake, for the SPHP personnel are highly trained police professionals. Had they been permitted to provide protection during the visit to Paris, assassins and the very aggressive French paparazzi would have been kept at bay. After making the aforementioned drive to the Villa Windsor, Diana went to the Ritz's hairdressing salon while Dodi visited Repossi's to collect the emerald and diamond engagement ring. Dodi had already told his step-uncle Hussein Yassin, who was at the Ritz for the weekend, that he and Diana were planning to marry. After returning to the hotel, Dodi also telephoned the news to Hussein's niece Joumana.

The couple left the Ritz at seven o'clock for the drive to Dodi's apartment in order to dress for dinner, with bodyguards Kez Wingfield and Trevor Rees-Jones following in Dodi's Land Rover – a clear security risk if the two vehicles had become separated. Arriving at the apartment, a clearly frightened Diana was jostled by an aggressive crowd of paparazzi. It was evident that the planned dinner at the Chez Benoit restaurant was out of the question because of the paparazzi's reckless behavior, so the couple returned to the Ritz, where they again had to force their way through a crowd of paparazzi and had dinner in their suite.

Security cameras revealed several men in the crowd outside the Ritz who had loitered in the vicinity for much of the day. Former Scotland Yard Chief Superintendent John McNamara, who later was appointed by Mohamed Al Fayed to head an investigation into the crash, identified these loiterers as members of British and foreign intelligence agencies.

Henri Paul returned to the Ritz shortly after 10:00PM after an absence of three hours and was asked to meet Dodi in his suite for further instructions. After the meeting with Henri Paul, Dodi notified the hotel night manager Thierry Rocher, that the couple planned to return to Dodi's apartment for the night and instructed the night manager to arrange for a limo to be brought to the rear exit of the Ritz shortly after midnight. He explained that Henri Paul would drive them to the apartment and that the two limos used earlier in the day were to remain parked out front as decoys.

Henri Paul contacted bodyguards Trevor Rees-Jones and Kez Wingfield who were waiting for further instructions and told the pair that he would be driving Diana and Dodi back to the apartment without bodyguards. Rees-Jones made it clear that he would not tolerate such a dangerous violation of security procedure. Dodi came out of his suite at that moment and confirmed Paul's comments that bodyguards were not necessary for the short trip. Rees-Jones remained firm and Dodi relented, agreeing that Rees-Jones could accompany them, but refused to permit a back-up vehicle to follow. Wingfield later claimed that he then tried to reason with Dodi, pointing out that security would be improved through the use of a back-up vehicle. Dodi insisted that his father had approved the arrangement. Dodi's father later stated that he was unaware of such a plan.

The black Mercedes S280 driven by Henri Paul, with Diana and Dodi in the rear and Trevor Rees-Jones in the front passenger seat, left from the back exit of the Ritz and proceeded at a normal speed along the rue Cambon, then turned right onto the rue Castiglione. Meanwhile, the Mercedes 600 and Range Rover decoy vehicles left from the front entrance of the Ritz for the five-minute drive to Dodi's apartment. As the Mercedes conveying Diana and Dodi drove away from the hotel, several photographers who had been monitoring the back entrance of the Ritz alerted the paparazzi waiting outside the hotel's front entrance that the lovers had given them the slip, prompting the paparazzi to belatedly give chase.

Arriving at the Place de la Concorde, instead of turning right onto the Champs Elysées as one normally would do to take the most direct route to Dodi's apartment, Henri Paul continued in a southerly direction towards the river Seine. Running a red traffic light, he rapidly accelerated and entered the Cours la Reine freeway, leaving the pursuing paparazzi far behind. This particular freeway passes through the Pont d'Alma tunnel where the fatal crash occurred.

Twenty-nine year old cook Eric Petel claims that he was the first person to reach the crash scene. According to the Reuters News Service, Petel stated that he was traveling at seventy miles per hour on his motorcycle when the Mercedes transporting Diana and Dodi overtook him while flashing its headlights. Petel claimed that he stopped at the crash scene, realized that the female passenger was Diana, and then rode to the nearest police station to report the accident. As well, Petel claimed that there was no other vehicle either in front of or behind the Mercedes at the time of the crash, nor had any paparazzi arrived during the time that he was in the tunnel.

Petel's account suggests that no other vehicle was involved in the crash. This is totally at odds with the statements made to the police by other eyewitnesses and the fact that the paparazzi were at most only a few hundred yards behind the Mercedes as it entered the tunnel. If Petel was the only eyewitness to the event, he could have sold his account to the tabloids for a considerable sum of money, yet he waited five months before going public with his story. Moreover, he released his account exactly the same weekend that the book *Death of a Princess* was released.

This book raised the possibility that a motorcycle and a white Fiat Uno observed by other eyewitnesses were involved in the crash. According to the police, damage at the crash scene demonstrated that another vehicle had been involved, implying that Petel's story lacks credibility. Moreover, there is no record of Petel reporting the incident to the police, suggesting that Petel's account was a lie perpetrated to misdirect attention away from the claim made in *Death of a Princess* that other vehicles were involved in the crash.

A married couple from Rouen was later interviewed by the Rouen police and the husband stated that as he entered the tunnel, he saw in his rearview mirror that the Mercedes was behind him with a motorcycle ridden by two persons on its left. The motorcycle suddenly swerved in front of the car and there was a flash of light "like a searchlight." He then heard a crash as he was exiting the tunnel.

The husband stopped the car, but his wife urged him to leave the crash scene fearing terrorists. Curiously, the husband later changed his story, claiming to the *Sunday People* newspaper that it was he who had swerved in front of the motorcycle thus causing the crash. Strangely, his wife still insisted that her husband's first account was the correct version, which also is corroborated by other eyewitnesses.

According to fifty-three year old François Levy, he was ahead of the Mercedes in the Alma tunnel. There was a motorcycle on the limo's left, which pulled ahead, then swerved into the Mercedes' lane. Of special importance is Levy's statement that as the motorcycle swerved and prior to the driver losing control of the limo, there was a flash of light. Levy said that he heard the crash as he was exiting the tunnel. British secretary Brenda Wells, a resident of Champigny sur Marne, who was returning to her residence after a party, corroborates his story. She stated that: "A motorbike with two men forced me off the road. It was following a big car. Afterwards in the tunnel there were very strong lights like flashes." She added that she stopped her car at the crash scene and several men on motorcycles arrived and began taking photographs.

Jean-Pascal Peyret and his wife heard an impact followed by a loud crash as they were exiting the Alma tunnel. He said that immediately after the crash a motorcycle overtook his vehicle. When he reported the incident to the police he was told that they were expecting him. This startling comment suggests that the surveillance camera at the tunnel entrance was functioning, enabling the police to read Peyret's license plate, thus contradicting the investigative team's claim that the camera wasn't working at the time of the crash.

Two off-duty chauffeurs who were standing near the tunnel entrance observed that Henri Paul downshifted in order to overtake a car that was attempting to slow down the limo. They also noticed a motorcycle in hot pursuit of the Mercedes.

California businessman Gary Anderson was a passenger in a taxi that was overtaken by the Mercedes, which was closely followed by two motorcycles. He stated that one of the motorcycles was being driven "aggressively and dangerously." According to Anderson, the motorcycle overtook the limo then swerved in front of it. A chauffeur and an engineer both told police that they witnessed two men on a motorcycle pursuing the Mercedes in a dangerous manner as the limo was approaching the tunnel.

In a newspaper interview, one witness said that he saw a car deliberately force the limo into the left hand lane as it entered the Alma tunnel. Another more detailed account of the same incident was provided in the official statement of off duty police officer David Laurent. The policeman was driving on the same freeway when a white Fiat Uno sped past him, heading in the same direction. As he approached the Alma tunnel, he saw the same car moving very slowly, as if the driver was waiting for someone.

At the time Henri Paul lost control of the limo, Dr. Frederic Mailliez was approaching the Alma tunnel in the eastbound lanes. The doctor was employed by S.O.S. Medicins, an emergency medical service owned by French insurance companies, and stopped at the crash scene where he administered oxygen to the injured Diana. Mailliez later made conflicting statements to the news media concerning Diana's injuries, initially stating "She looked pretty fine." During a CNN television interview he remarked: "I thought this woman had a chance."

A few weeks later, when interviewed by the French medical magazine **Impact Quotidien**, he contradicted his earlier statements, claiming "There was no way, no chance for her."

This latter statement is at variance with the comment made by Dr. Jean-Marc Martino, who was in charge of the ambulance crew that transported Diana to hospital. He stated that he considered her condition as: "severe but not critical."

Diana allegedly underwent two heart attacks between the time of the crash and her arrival at the hospital. Unlike ambulances typically used in most countries, the ambulances of the French emergency service SAMU are actually sophisticated mobile surgical units. It would therefore be readily apparent to the ambulance crew attending to Diana's injuries that a heart specialist would be required after her arrival at the hospital.

Despite radio communication between the ambulance crew and the hospital staff, no heart specialist was present when the ambulance finally arrived at the hospital, nor had a heart lung machine been prepared ready for Diana's surgery if required. Still, French authorities had found time to summon French politicians, police and British ambassador Sir Michael Jay to the hospital prior to the arrival of the ambulance. Inexplicably, one hour and 46 minutes elapsed between the time of the crash and the arrival of the ambulance at the hospital.

The cause of Diana's death was attributed to a ruptured pulmonary vein that resulted in massive internal bleeding. Physicians all over the globe later spoke out against the ambulance crew for taking such an inordinate amount of time to transport Diana to the hospital, which only entailed a four-mile journey. Had she been transported sooner, they claimed, her chances of survival would have been greatly improved.

Dr. Patrick Goldstein, a vice president of SAMU, defended the ambulance crew's actions, claiming: "Diana had no chance of making it." Perhaps Dr. Goldstein is unaware that President Ronald Reagan, like Diana, also sustained a damaged pulmonary vein when he was shot, yet survived due to the expeditious manner in which he was rushed to hospital.

Diana was pronounced dead at 4:00AM on the same day that the crash occurred. A strange incident occurred later that morning which clouds the issue of whether or not Diana was pregnant and also suggests an unlawful course of action on the part of the Windsors and French authorities. It is a violation of French law to embalm a body prior to an autopsy, or to embalm a body without the consent of the next of kin, yet a partial embalming of Diana's body above the waist was performed prior to an autopsy and without the consent of the Spencer family.

The order to perform the embalming came from the office of Prince Charles at St. James's Palace. This order was a blatant violation of French law since the prince was no longer Diana's husband. Strangely, a hospital spokesperson claimed that a sample of Diana's blood was never taken, which is very odd since they would have needed a sample in order to determine Diana's blood type prior to administering the blood transfusions purportedly given her.

In order to find a scapegoat for the crash, the French investigative team headed by Commander Jean-Claude Mules claimed that the aggressive pursuit of the limo by the paparazzi caused the crash. When it became public knowledge that the paparazzi were several hundred yards behind the limo at the time of the crash, the investigators, aided by the British and French news media, focused their attention on driver Henri Paul, claiming that it was his drunkenness and reckless driving which resulted in the crash. At the present time, the official position adopted by the French authorities is that the crash resulted from both the aggressiveness of the paparazzi and the drunkenness of Henri Paul, despite all the eyewitness evidence to the contrary.

What really caused the crash and was it accidental or murder? With the exception of Eric Petel's questionable account of the crash, the consensus of eleven other eyewitness accounts suggests that after leaving the Place de la Concorde, Henri Paul accelerated, leaving the paparazzi behind, but was closely pursued by one or possibly two motorcyclists.

Approaching the Pont d'Alma tunnel, one of the motorcycles aggressively cut in front of the limo, forcing Henri Paul to swerve into the right lane in order to avoid a collision, only to be impeded by a white Fiat Uno barely moving. In taking evasive action, the limo veered to the left, clipping the Fiat and damaging its left taillight.

Regaining control of the limo, Paul began turning to the right, with the motorcycle in the left hand lane and slightly ahead of the limo. At that precise moment, a passenger on the motorcycle apparently triggered a strobe light that temporarily blinded and disoriented Henri Paul, causing the fatal crash. The motorcycle slowed then sped away accompanied by the damaged Fiat Uno and followed by a white Mercedes.

Since that time, evidence has been uncovered that shows Princess Diana's death was not an accident, in fact, Diana herself was certain that she was targeted for death by the very people who were supposed to be protecting her. Paul Burrell, Diana's butler, has revealed a letter from her in which she said she feared that someone was "planning an accident in my car." The sworn testimony of former MI6 agent Richard Tomlinson describes his knowledge of a MI6 plot to assassinate Serbian leader President Slobodan Milosevic with a very similar scheme.

Tomlinson states that he firmly believes that there exists documents held by the British Secret Intelligence Service (MI6) that would yield important new evidence into the cause and circumstances leading to the deaths of the Princess of Wales, Mr Dodi Al Fayed, and M. Henri Paul in Paris in August 1997.

I was employed by MI6 between September 1991 and April 1995. During that time, I saw various documents that I believe would provide new evidence and new leads into the investigation into these deaths. I also heard various rumours which though I was not able to see supporting documents I am confident were based on solid fact.

In 1992, I was working in the Eastern European Controllerate of MI6 and I was peripherally involved in a large and complicated operation to smuggle advanced Soviet weaponry out of the then disintegrating and disorganised remnants of the Soviet Union. During 1992, I spent several days reading the substantial files on this operation. These files contain a wide miscellany of contact notes, telegrams, intelligence reports, photographs etc, from which it was possible to build up a detailed understanding of the operation.

The operation involved a large cast of officers and agents of MI6. One more than one occasion, meetings between various figures in the operation took place at the Ritz Hotel, Place de Vendome, Paris. There were in the file several intelligence reports on these meetings, which had been written by one of the MI6 officers based in Paris at the time (identified in the file only by a coded designation).

The source of the information was an informant in the Ritz Hotel, who again was identified in the files only by a code number. The MI6 officer paid the informant in cash for his information. I became curious to learn more about the identity of this particular informant, because his number cropped up several times and he seemed to have extremely good access to the goings on in the Ritz Hotel. I therefore ordered this informant's personal file from MI6's central file registry.

When I read this new file, I was not at all surprised to learn that the informant was a security officer of the Ritz Hotel. Intelligence services always target the security officers of important hotels because they have such good access to intelligence. I remember, however, being mildly surprised that the nationality of this informant was French, and this stuck in my memory, because it is rare that MI6 succeeds in recruiting a French informer. I cannot claim that I remember from this reading of the file that the name of this person was Henri Paul, but I have no doubt with the benefit of hindsight that this was he.

Although I did not subsequently come across Henri Paul again during my time in MI6, I am confident that the relationship between he and MI6 would have continued until his death, because MI6 would never willingly relinquish control over such a well-placed informant. I am sure that the personal file of Henri Paul will therefore contain notes of meetings between him and his MI6 controlling officer right up until the point of his death. I firmly believe that these files will contain evidence of crucial importance to the circumstances and causes of the incident that killed M. Paul, together with the Princess of Wales and Dodi Al Fayed.

The most senior undeclared officer in the local MI6 station would normally control an informant of M. Paul's usefulness and seniority. Officers declared to the local counter-intelligence service (in this case the Directorate de Surveillance Territoire, or DST) would not be used to control such an informant, because it might lead to the identity of the informant becoming known to the local intelligence services.

In Paris at the time of M. Paul's death, there were two relatively experienced but undeclared MI6 officers. The first was Mr. Nicholas John Andrew LANGMAN, born 1960. The second was Mr. Richard David SPEARMAN, again born in 1960. I firmly believe that either one or both of these officers will be well acquainted with M Paul, and most probably also met M. Paul shortly before his death. I believe that either or both of these officers will have knowledge that will be of crucial importance in establishing the sequence of events leading up to the deaths of M. Paul, Dodi Al Fayed and the Princess of Wales.

Mr. Spearman in particular was an extremely well connected and influential officer, because he had been, prior to his appointment in Paris, the personal secretary to the Chief of MI6 Mr. David Spedding. As such, he would have been privy to even the most confidential of MI6 operations. I believe that there may well be significance in the fact that Mr. Spearman was posted to Paris in the month immediately before the deaths.

Later in 1992, as the civil war in the former Yugoslavia became increasingly topical, I started to work primarily on operations in Serbia. During this time, I became acquainted with Dr. Nicholas Bernard Frank FISHWICK, born 1958, the MI6 officer who at the time was in charge of planning Balkan operations.

During one meeting with Dr. Fishwick, he casually showed to me a three-page document that on closer inspection turned out to be an outline plan to assassinate the Serbian leader President Slobodan Milosevic.

The plan was fully typed, and attached to a yellow "minute board," signifying that this was a formal and accountable document. It will therefore still be in existence.

Fishwick had annotated that the document be circulated to the following senior MI6 officers: Maurice KENDWRICK-PIERCEY, then head of Balkan operations, John RIDDE, then the security officer for Balkan operations, the SAS liaison officer to MI6 (designation MODA/SO, but I have forgotten his name), the head of the Eastern European Controllerate (then Richard FLETCHER) and finally Alan PETTY, the personal secretary to the then Chief of MI6, Colin McCOLL.

This plan contained a political justification for the assassination of Milosevic, followed by three outline proposals on how to achieve this objective.

I firmly believe that the third of these scenarios contained information that could be useful in establishing the causes of death of Henri Paul, the Princess of Wales, and Dodi Al Fayed.

This third scenario suggested that Milosevic could be assassinated by causing his personal limousine to crash.

Dr. Fishwick proposed to arrange the crash in a tunnel, because the proximity of concrete close to the road would ensure that the crash would be sufficiently violent to cause death or serious injury, and would also reduce the possibility that there might be independent, casual witnesses.

Dr. Fishwick suggested that one way to cause the crash might be to disorientate the chauffeur using a strobe flash gun, a device which is occasionally deployed by special forces to, for example, disorientate helicopter pilots or terrorists, and about which MI6 officers are briefed about during their rigorous training.

In short, this scenario bore remarkable similarities to the circumstances and witness accounts of the crash that killed the Princess of Wales, Dodi Al Fayed, and Henri Paul. I firmly believe that this document should be yielded by MI6 to the Judge investigating these deaths, and would provide further leads that he could follow.

During my service in MI6, I also learnt unofficially and second-hand something of the links between MI6 and the Royal Household. MI6 are frequently and routinely asked by the Royal Household (usually via the Foreign Office) to provide intelligence on potential threats to members of the Royal Family whilst on overseas trips.

This service would frequently extend to asking friendly intelligence services (such as the CIA) to place members of the Royal Family under discrete surveillance, ostensibly for their own protection.

This was particularly the case for the Princess of Wales, who often insisted on doing without overt personal protection, even on overseas trips. Although contact between MI6 and the Royal Household was officially only via the Foreign Office, I learnt while in MI6 that there was unofficial direct contact between certain senior and influential MI6 officers and senior members of the Royal Household.

I did not see any official papers on this subject, but I am confident that the information is correct. I firmly believe that MI6 documents would yield substantial leads on the nature of their links with the Royal Household, and would yield vital information about MI6 surveillance on the Princess in the days leading to her death.

I also learnt while in MI6 that one of the "paparazzi" photographers who routinely followed the Princess of Wales was a member of "UKN", a small corps of part-time MI6 agents who provide miscellaneous services to MI6 such as surveillance and photography expertise. I do not know the identity of this photographer, or whether he was one of the photographers present at the time of the fatal incident.

However, I am confident that examination of UKN records would yield the identity of this photographer, and would enable the inquest to eliminate or further investigate that potential line of enquiry.

On Friday August 28 1998, I gave much of this information to Judge Hervé Stephan, the French investigative Judge in charge of the inquest into the accident. The lengths that MI6, the CIA and the DST have taken to deter me giving this evidence and subsequently to stop me talking about it, suggests that they have something to hide.

On Friday 31 July 1998, shortly before my appointment with Judge Hervé Stephan, the DST arrested me in my Paris hotel room. Although I have no record of violent conduct I was arrested with such ferocity and at gunpoint that I received a broken rib.

I was taken to the headquarters of the DST, and interrogated for 38 hours. Despite my repeated requests, I was never given any justification for the arrest and was not shown the arrest warrant. Even though I was released without charge, the DST confiscated from me my laptop computer and Psion organiser. They illegally gave these to MI6 who took them back to the UK. They were not returned for six months, which is illegal and caused me great inconvenience and financial cost.

On Friday 7th August 1998 I boarded a Qantas flight at Auckland International airport, New Zealand, for a flight to Sydney, Australia where I was due to give a television interview to the Australian Channel Nine television company. I was in my seat, awaiting take off, when an official boarded the plane and told me to get off.

At the airbridge, he told me that the airline had received a fax "from Canberra" saying that there was a problem with my travel papers. I immediately asked to see the fax, but I was told that: "it was not possible". I believe that this is because it didn't exist. This action was a ploy to keep me in New Zealand so that the New Zealand police could take further action against me. I had been back in my Auckland hotel room for about half an hour when the New Zealand police and NZSIS, the New Zealand Secret Intelligence Service, raided me.

After being detained and searched for about three hours, they eventually confiscated from me all my remaining computer equipment that the French DST had not succeeded in taking from me. Again, I didn't get some of these items back until six months later.

Moreover, shortly after I had given this evidence to Judge Stephan, I was invited to talk about this evidence in a live television interview on America's NBC television channel.

I flew from Geneva to JFK airport on Sunday 30 August to give the interview in New York on the following Monday morning. Shortly after arrival at John F Kennedy airport, the captain of the Swiss Air flight told all passengers to return to their seats.

Four US Immigration authority officers entered the plane, came straight to my seat, asked for my passport as identity, and then frogmarched me off the plane.

I was taken to the immigration detention centre, photographed, fingerprinted, manacled by my ankle to a chair for seven hours, served with deportation papers and then returned on the next available plane to Geneva. I was not allowed to make any telephone calls to the representatives of NBC awaiting me in the airport. The US Immigration Officers, who were all sympathetic to my situation and apologised for treating me so badly, admitted that they were acting under instructions from the CIA.

In January of this year, I booked a chalet in the village of Samoens in the French Alps for a ten-day snowboarding holiday with my parents. I picked up my parents from Geneva airport in a hire car on the evening of January 8, and set off for the French border.

At the French customs post, our car was stopped and I was detained. Four officers from the DST held me for four hours. At the end of this interview, I was served with the deportation papers below (exhibit 2), and ordered to return to Switzerland. Note that in the papers, my supposed destination has been changed from "Chamonix" to "Samoens". This is because when first questioned by a junior DST officer, I told him that my destination was "Chamonix". When a senior officer arrived an hour or so later, he crossed out the word and changed it to "Samoens", without ever even asking or confirming this with me. I believe this is because MI6 had told them of my true destination, having learnt the information through surveillance on my parent's telephone in the UK.

My banning from France is entirely illegal under European law. I have a British passport and am entitled to travel freely within the European Union. MI6 have "done a deal" with the DST to have me banned, and have not used any recognised legal mechanism to deny my rights to freedom of travel. I believe that the DST and MI6 have banned me from France because they wanted to prevent me from giving further evidence to Judge Stephan's inquest, which at the time, I was planning to do.

Whatever MI6's role in the events leading to the death of the Princess of Wales, Dodi Al Fayed and Henri Paul, I am absolutely certain that there is substantial evidence in their files that would provide crucial evidence in establishing the exact causes of this tragedy.

I believe that they have gone to considerable lengths to obstruct the course of justice by interfering with my freedom of speech and travel, and this in my view confirms my belief that they have something to hide. I believe that the protection given to MI6 files under the Official Secrets Act should be set aside in the public interest in uncovering once and for all the truth behind these dramatic and historically momentous events.

The body count associated with Princess Diana's death continued with the strange "suicide" of Jean-Paul "James" Andanson, a 54-year-old millionaire photographer, who was among the paparazzi stalking Princess Diana and Dodi Fayed during the week before their deaths. On May 5, 2000, police in the south of France found a badly burned body inside the wreckage of a car, deep in the woods near Nantes. The body was so charred that it took police nearly a month before DNA tests confirmed that the dead man was Andanson.

From the day of the fatal crash in the Place de l'Alma tunnel, Andanson had been at the center of the controversy. At least seven eyewitnesses to the crash said that they saw a white Fiat Uno and a motorcycle speed out of the tunnel, seconds after the crash. Forensic tests have confirmed that a white Fiat Uno collided with the Mercedes carrying Diana and Dodi, and that this collision was a significant factor in the crash.

Andanson had been in and around Sardinia during the last week of August 1997, as Diana and Dodi vacationed in the Mediterranean. He joined several dozen other paparazzi who were stalking the couple's every move. He was back in France on Aug. 30, the day that Diana and Dodi flew to Paris.

For reasons that he never revealed, sometime before dawn on Aug. 31, 1997, less than six hours after the crash in the Alma tunnel, Andanson boarded a flight at Orly Airport near Paris, bound for Corsica. Andanson claimed that he was not in Paris earlier in the evening, when the crash occurred, but he never produced any evidence to prove he was not in the city.

Andanson's wife, Elizabeth, claimed that she had been at home with her husband all night, at their country home, Le Manoir de la Bergerie, in Cher, until he abruptly left for Orly, at 3:45 a.m., to catch the crack-of-dawn flight to Corsica. Mrs. Anderson later admitted to reporters and police that her husband was constantly on the run, and she could have been mistaken about the night in question.

What makes Andanson's precise itinerary the night of the fatal crash so vital was that he owned and drove a white Fiat Uno. The car was repainted shortly after the Aug. 31, 1997 Alma tunnel crash, and was sold by Andanson in October 1997. Although the official report of the French authorities investigating the crash concluded that Andanson's car was not involved in the crash, French forensic reports said otherwise.

One report in the files of Judge Herve Stephan, the chief investigating magistrate in the Diana-Dodi crash probe, described the tests on Andanson's Fiat: "The comparative analysis of the infrared spectra characterizing the vehicle's original paint, reference Bianco 210, and the trace on the side-view mirror of the Mercedes shows that their absorption bands are identical." In laymen's terms, the paint scratches from the Fiat found on the side-view mirror of the Mercedes were identical to the paint samples taken from the matching spot on Andanson's Fiat.

The report continued: "The comparative analysis between the infrared spectra characterizing the black polymer taken from the vehicle's fender, and the trace taken from the door of the Mercedes, show that their absorption bands are identical."

Strange and Unexplained Deaths at the Hands of the Secret Government

John Macnamara, the Harrods director of security, and a retired senior Scotland Yard supervisor of investigations, told reporters: "Mr. Andanson had for some time been a prime suspect who had relentlessly pursued Diana and Dodi prior to their arrival in Paris. We have always believed that Andanson was at the scene and that more investigation should have been done into his possible involvement."

Macnamara added, "We believe that his death is no coincidence and that this is a line of inquiry which may help to discover the truth. Was Mr. Andanson killed because of what he knew? That is a question we want answered."

Andanson's widow Elizabeth, and their son James have rejected the idea that Andanson's death was suicide. Sources close to the family said that they have pressed French officials to conduct a murder investigation into Andanson's death that occurred 400-miles from his home. The sources dismiss bogus "marital problems" rumors stressing that Andanson was in high spirits over his new job with the Sipa Agency.

Adding fuel to the fire of suspicion, shortly after midnight on June 16, 2000, just one week after Andanson's death was first made public, three masked men armed with handguns, broke into the Sipa office in Paris, shooting a security guard in the foot. The three assailants dismantled all of the security cameras in the office, and proceeded to enter several specific offices, clearly aware of exactly what they were looking for. They made off with several cameras, laptop computers, and computer hard drives.

The three invaders spent three hours in the office, holding employees hostage. According to one of the hostages, the men were never concerned about the French police arriving at the scene. This hostage was convinced that the three "burglars" were themselves working for some branch of the French Secret Service. Furthermore, the source confirmed that Andanson had worked for French and, undoubtedly, British security agencies.

The owner of Sipa, Sipa Hioglou, told police that he suspected that the raid had nothing to do with Andanson, and was done on behalf of a disgruntled celebrity who was angry that her picture had been taken by a Sipa paparazzo without her permission. However, other Sipa employees have told the police that the idea that Andanson committed suicide was preposterous, and that they suspect that the break-in was related to his death.

Evidence has recently come to light, that within hours of the crash, British and French secret service agencies carried out a series of break-ins at the homes and offices of several photo-agency personnel, in a desperate search for photos of the crash site that may have been transmitted in the hours immediately after the Alma tunnel collision, and before word of Princess Diana's death was made public.

The death of Andanson may very well signal a new, deadly turn in the cover-up of the death of Princess Diana. It is reminiscent of the pile of corpses that littered the landscape following the assassination of President John F. Kennedy, when scores of individuals with knowledge about the President's death, died under mysterious circumstances.

CHAPTER TWO
Innocent Bystanders

The assassination of President John F. Kennedy brought with it an industry of conspiracy researchers and writers, all with their own favorite theories, perpetrators and motives. The list of possible conspirators is far-reaching and diverse, ranging from such people and groups as Vice-President Lyndon B. Johnson, Richard Nixon, right-wing extremists, Fidel Castro, the Russians, the mafia, the CIA and or FBI, former Nazi's, the Illuminati, etc. It seems that everyone had a motive and means to want President Kennedy dead.

What has escaped the notice of all but the most dedicated researchers is the fact that dozens of eyewitnesses, and others supposedly involved in the plot to kill Kennedy, have allegedly died under mysterious circumstances. Those who scoff at the idea that a conspiracy existed to murder the President shrug-off any evidence that there seemed to be a systematic, underlying plot to remove those who could dispute the official pronouncement that Kennedy was assassinated by a lone gunman.

One of the first journalists to actively investigate the Kennedy assassination was Penn Jones Jr., an editor for the Texas newspaper ***The Midlothian Mirror***. Jones began researching the assassination the day it happened. He had been at the International Trade Mart where the luncheon for JFK was going to be held. When he first heard the news that Kennedy had been shot in Dealey Plaza, he immediately drove to the scene and began to talk with people who had witnessed the assassination.

Jones, an outspoken critic of the Warren Report, began to catalog the unsettling pattern among those people whose lives, in one way or another, were connected with the assassination of JFK, and who all shared the same fate of meeting unusual and untimely deaths. In the forward to his ***Forgive My Grief***, Volume 3, 1969, (there were four volumes in all) he wrote:

> It has always been difficult for a democracy to return to democracy after a prolonged period of dictatorship that always comes with war. Few people remember or even know of the great struggle which went on in the United States after World War I when red baiting got its start. Civil rights were violated on a mass scale during and after World War I until civilian control of the country was again established.
>
> We never made the return to democracy after World War II. The changes were more subtle this time, but just as deadly. Much of the take-over by the military was hidden behind the attacks on the military by Senator Joe McCarthy. But the military encroachment apparently is permanent.
>
> The military power grab was the real key behind the assassination of President John F. Kennedy. A struggle which is already lost and is confirmed by the long list of strange deaths

which have been recorded in *The Midlothian Mirror* in *Forgive My Grief*, Volumes. I and II, and in this book.

People in the United States pretend that President Kennedy was killed by a lone individual. All the rest of the world knows this is not true. It is really too late to continue to debate whether or not a conspiracy does exist to kill liberal leaders in this country. After the deaths of President Kennedy, Senator Robert Kennedy, Martin Luther King, Malcolm X, Ambassador Stevenson and Medgar Evers, conspiracy debates should be ended.

A conspiracy does exist. Not only are liberal leaders killed when they threaten the establishment, at least sixty-eight others have had to die in order to keep the truth about the assassinations from getting out. The really tragic fact in the United States is that the citizenry is uninformed or misinformed. The public has not read the record of these killing's, therefore our people float lethargically in ignorance. And ignorance is cancer to democracy.

Many witnesses died in the thirteen-year period following the Kennedy assassination, mostly of unnatural causes. In fact, rumors were circulating around Dallas only weeks after the assassination that witnesses were on a "hit-list" to silence them before they had a chance to talk with investigators.

It was already well known among reporters who were conducting their own research into the assassination that many witnesses were complaining that their testimonies were being discredited, taken out of context or actually changed by the Dallas Police and the FBI. Those who offered substantial evidence against Oswald being the lone gunman were quickly silenced, taking their knowledge with them to the grave.

The list of names and the circumstances of unusual deaths stretch from Oswald himself to innocent bystanders and mob associates alike. In the five years after Kennedy's death, nearly 60 people with direct knowledge of the assassination died untimely deaths.

These mysterious deaths have also succeeded in silencing other potential witnesses who feared for their lives. Why would Jack Ruby, a known mob figure, essentially throw his own life away to kill Oswald on national TV if it were really, as he says, out of sorrow for Jacqueline Kennedy? Why would Ruby insist until his death that the real truth had not come out about the assassination? Why wasn't his action officially recognized for what it was, a standard organized crime technique for silencing witnesses?

Jim Marrs, in his 1989 book ***CROSSFIRE***, writes that the CIA has gone to great lengths to discredit the idea of mysterious deaths plaguing assassination witnesses. A 1967 memo from CIA headquarters to station chiefs advised: "Such vague accusations as that 'more than 10 people have died mysteriously' can always be explained in some rational way: e.g., the individuals concerned have for the most part died of natural causes; the Warren Commission staff questioned 418 witnesses, the FBI conducted 25,000 interviews, and in such a large group, a certain number of deaths are to be expected."

Strange and Unexplained Deaths at the Hands of the Secret Government

Testifying before the Church Committee in 1975, CIA technicians told of a variety of TWEP technology – Terminate With Extreme Prejudice – that cannot be detected in a postmortem examination. One recently declassified CIA document, a letter from an Agency consultant to a CIA officer, states:

> You will recall that I mentioned that the local circumstances under which a given means might be used might suggest the technique to be used in that case. I think the gross divisions in presenting this subject might be:
> (1) Bodies left with no hope of the cause of death being determined by the most complete autopsy and chemical examinations.
> (2) Bodies left in such circumstances as to simulate accidental death.
> (3) Bodies left in such circumstances as to simulate suicidal death.
> (4) Bodies left with residue that simulates those caused by natural diseases.

The letter goes on to show that undetected murders do not have to be the result of sophisticated chemicals. It states:

> There are two techniques which I believe should be mentioned since they require no special equipment besides a strong arm and the will to do such a job. These would be either to smother the victim with a pillow or to strangle him with a wide piece of cloth such as a bath towel. In such cases, there are no specific anatomic changes to indicate the cause of death..

While it is obvious that the CIA, and hence the mob through operatives who work for both, has the capability of killing, it is less well known that the Agency has developed drugs to induce cancer. Recall that Jack Ruby died of sudden lung cancer just as he had been granted a new trial.

A 1952 CIA memo reported on the cancer-causing effects of beryllium: "This is certainly the most toxic inorganic element and it produces a peculiar fibrotic tumor at the site of local application. The amount necessary to produce these tumors is a few micrograms."

Local law-enforcement officers and coroners are not equipped, either by training or by inclination, to detect deaths induced by such sophisticated means. They look for signs of a struggle, evidence of a break-in, bruises, or marks on the victim. With no evidence to the contrary, many deaths are ruled suicide or accident. Others are ruled due to natural causes, such as heart attack.

It is interesting to note how the deaths are grouped. Many of the earliest deaths came during the time of the Warren Commission investigation or just afterwards.

More deaths took place in the late 1960s as New Orleans District Attorney Jim Garrison was launching his investigation. Other suspicious deaths occurred during the mid-1970s, as the Senate Intelligence Committee was looking into assassinations by U.S. intelligence agencies. And finally, another group of deaths came around 1977, just as the House Select Committee on Assassinations was gearing up its investigation.

It is thought that the first person to die linked to the Kennedy assassination was Karyn Kupcinet. A few days before the assassination, Karyn Kupcinet, age 23, was trying to place a long distance telephone call from the Los Angeles area. According to reports, the long distance operator heard Miss Kupcinet scream into the telephone that: "President Kennedy was going to be killed." Karyn's body was discovered on November 30, 1963. Police estimated that she had been dead for two days. *The New York Times* reported that she had been strangled. Her actor boyfriend, Andrew Prine was the main suspect but he was never charged with the murder and the crime remains unsolved.

Some researchers claim that there was a link between the death of Kupcinet and the assassination of JFK. It is said that the conspirators were trying to frighten off her father, journalist Irv Kupcinet from telling what he knew about the case.

Before President Kennedy came to Dallas, two men who worked for Jack Ruby threw stripper Rose Cherami out of a speeding car and abandoned her by the side of the road. She claimed that she knew of a plot to kill the President, and in a later statement she also said that Rack Ruby and Lee Oswald were involved in a sexual Liaison. Cherami was killed in a mysterious hit and run accident in 1965.

Grant Stockdale, a close friend of President Kennedy died on December 2, 1963 when he fell (or was pushed) from his office on the thirteenth story of the Dupont Building in Miami. Stockdale did not leave a suicide note but his friend, George Smathers, claimed that he had become depressed as a result of the death of the President.

It later became known that four days after the assassination, Stockdale flew to Washington and talked with Robert and Edward Kennedy. On his return Stockdale told several of his friends that "the world was closing in." On the first of December he spoke to his attorney, William Frates, who later recalled: "He started talking. It didn't make much sense. He said something about 'those guys' trying to get him, then about the assassination."

Shortly after dark on Sunday night, November 24, 1963, after Jack Ruby had killed Lee Harvey Oswald, a meeting took place in Ruby's apartment in Oak Cliff, a suburb of Dallas, Texas. Five people were there. George Senator and Attorney Tom Howard were present and having a drink in the apartment when two newsmen arrived. The newsmen were Bill Hunter of the Long Beach California *Press Telegram* and Jim Koethe of the *Dallas Times* Herald. Attorney C.A. droby of Dallas arranged the meeting for the two newsmen, Jim Martin, a close friend of George Senator's, was also present at the apartment meeting.

Newspaper editor Penn Jones, Jr. asked Martin if he thought it was unusual for Senator to forget the meeting while testifying in Washington on April 22, 1964, since Bill Hunter, who was a newsman present at the meeting, was shot to death that very night. Martin said: "Oh, you're looking for a conspiracy, you'll never find it."

In the November 22, 1983 issue of **The Rebel**, Jones writes that Bill Hunter, a native of Dallas and an award-winning newsman in Long Beach, was on duty and reading a book in the police station called the "Public Safety Building." Two policemen going off duty came into the pressroom, and one policeman shot Hunter through the heart at a range officially ruled to be "no more than three feet." The policeman said he dropped his gun, and it fired as he picked it up, but the angle of the bullet caused him to change his story. He finally said he was playing a game of quick draw with his fellow officer. The other officer testified he had his back turned when the shooting took place.

Hunter, who covered the assassination for his paper, **The Long Beach Press Telegram** had written: "Within minutes of Ruby's execution of Oswald, before the eyes of millions watching television, at least two Dallas attorneys appeared to talk with him."

Hunter was quoting Tom Howard who died of a heart attack in Dallas a few months after Hunter's own death. Lawyer Tom Howard was observed acting strangely to his friends two days before his death. According to the newspapers, a "friend" took Howard to the hospital. No autopsy was performed.

An unknown assailant killed **Dallas Times Herald** reporter Jim Koethe with a karate chop to the throat just as he emerged from a shower in his apartment on Sept. 21, 1964. His murderer was not indicted.

What went on in that significant meeting in Ruby and Senator's apartment? Few are left to tell. There is no one in authority to ask the question, since the Warren Commission has made its final report, and the House Select Committee has closed its investigation.

Dorothy Kilgallen was another reporter who died strangely and suddenly after her involvement in the Kennedy assassination. Kilgallen is the only journalist who was granted a private interview with Jack Ruby after he killed Oswald. Judge Joe B. Brown granted the interview during the course of the Ruby trial in Dallas – to the intense anger of the hundreds of other newspapers present.

Kilgallen stated that she was "going to break this case wide open." She never did. Instead, she was found dead on November 8, 1965. Her autopsy report took eight days. She was 52 years old. Two days later Mrs. Earl T. Smith, a close friend and confidant of Kilgallen's, died of undetermined causes.

Tom Howard, who died of a heart attack, was a good friend of District Attorney Henry Wade, although they often opposed each other in court. Howard was close to Ruby and other fringes of the Dallas underworld.

Like Ruby, Howard's life revolved around the police station, and it was not surprising when he and Ruby (toting his gun) showed up at the station on the evening of the assassination of President Kennedy. Nor was it unusual when Howard arrived at the jail shortly after Ruby shot Oswald, asking to see his old friend.

Howard was shown into a meeting room to see a bewildered Ruby who had not asked for a lawyer. For the next two days – until Ruby's brother, Earl, soured on him, and had Howard relieved – he was Jack Ruby's chief attorney and public spokesman.

Howard took to the publicity with enthusiasm, called a press conference, wheeled and dealed. He told newsmen the case was a: "once-in-a-lifetime chance," and that "speaking as a private citizen," he thought Ruby deserved a Congressional medal. He told the *Houston Post* that Ruby had been in the police station Friday night (Nov. 22, 1963) with a gun. Howard dickered with a national magazine for an Oswald murder story. Ruby's sister, Eva Grant, even accused Howard of leaking information to the DA. It was never quite clear whether Howard was working for Ruby or against him.

On March 27, 1965, Howard was taken to a hospital by an unidentified person and died there. He was 48. The doctor, without benefit of an autopsy, said he had suffered a heart attack. Some reporters and friends of Howard's were not so certain. Some said he was "bumped off."

Earlene Roberts was the plump widow who managed the rooming house where Lee Harvey Oswald was living under the name O.H. Lee. She testified before the Warren Commission that she saw Oswald come home around one o'clock, go to his room for three to four minutes and then walk out. A few minutes later, a mile away, officer J.D. Tippit was shot dead.

Mrs. Roberts testified that while Oswald was in his room, two uniformed cops pulled up in front of the rooming house and honked twice: "Just tit-tit," she said. The police department issued a report saying all patrol cars in the area, except Tippit's were accounted for.

After testifying in Dallas in April 1964, Mrs. Roberts was subjected to intensive police harassment. They visited her at all hours of the day and night. Earlene complained of being "worried to death" by the police. She died on January 9, 1966 in Parkland Hospital (the hospital where President Kennedy was taken). Police said she suffered a heart attack in her home. No autopsy was performed.

After the assassination of President Kennedy, Gary Underhill told his friend, Charlene Fitsimmons, that he was convinced that agents of the CIA had killed Kennedy. He also said: "Oswald is a patsy. They set him up. It's too much. The bastards have done something outrageous. They've killed the President! I've been listening and hearing things. I couldn't believe they'd get away with it, but they did!"

Underhill believed there was a connection between Executive Action, Fidel Castro and the death of John F. Kennedy: "They tried it in Cuba and they couldn't get away with it, right after the Bay of Pigs, but Kennedy wouldn't let them do it. And now he'd gotten wind of this and he was really going to blow the whistle on them. And they killed him!"

Gary Underhill told friends that he feared for his life: "I know who they are. That's the problem. They know I know. That's why I'm here. I can't stay in New York." Underhill was found dead on May 8, 1964. He had been shot in the head and it was officially ruled that he had committed suicide. However, in his book, *Destiny Betrayed*, James DiEugenio claimed that the bullet entered the right-handed Underhill's head behind the left ear.

On July 21, 1964, Dr. Mary Sherman was murdered in New Orleans. She had been stabbed in the heart, arm, leg and stomach. Her laboratory was also set on fire. The crime has never been solved. Later Edward T. Haslam published *Mary, Ferrie & the Monkey Virus: The Story of an Underground Medical Laboratory*.

In the book he argued that Sherman was working with David Ferrie. Haslam believed that this Central Intelligence Agency backed research involved disease intelligence gathering and cancer research using laboratory-made biological weapons. Haslam claimed this biological weapon was to be used against Cuba's Fidel Castro.

Judyth Baker later began giving interviews about involvement in an anti-Castro conspiracy. She claims that in 1963 she was recruited by Dr. Canute Michaelson to work with Dr. Alton Ochsner and Dr. Mary Sherman in a CIA secret project. This involved creating the means to insure Fidel Castro developed cancer.

In 1963 Judyth moved to New Orleans where she worked closely with others involved in this plot. This included Lee Harvey Oswald, David Ferrie, Clay Shaw and Guy Bannister. Later she claimed she began an affair with Oswald. The research into this biological weapon was carried out in the homes of Ferrie and Sherman. Oswald role in this conspiracy was to work as a courier. However, the project was suddenly abandoned in September 1963, and Oswald was ordered to Dallas.

Oswald kept in touch with Baker and in November 1963, he had been forced to join a plot to kill John F. Kennedy. Oswald believed that Mafia leader, Carlos Marcello and a CIA agent, David Atlee Phillips, was organizing the conspiracy. Oswald told Baker that he would do what he could to ensure that Kennedy was not killed. After the assassination of Kennedy and the arrest of Oswald, Baker received a phone call from Ferrie warning her that she would be killed if she told anyone about her knowledge of these events.

In 1963 Desmond FitzGerald was in charge of the CIA's Cuban Task Force. In this post he personally organized three different plots to assassinate Fidel Castro. According to Dick Russell, FitzGerald had a meeting in France with a Cuban code-named AM/LASH, finalizing a plan to eliminate Castro, at the same time John F. Kennedy was assassinated. FitzGerald died of a heart attack while playing tennis in Virginia on July 23, 1967.

Lisa Howard died at East Hampton, Long Island on July 4, 1965. It was officially reported that she had committed suicide. Apparently, she had taken one hundred Phenobarbitals. It was claimed she was depressed as a result of losing her job and suffering a miscarriage. At first no one associated Howard's death with the Kennedy assassination. However, it has recently emerged that Howard was involved in secret negotiations with Fidel Castro on behalf of Kennedy.

Winston Scott was the CIA's station chief in Mexico. Scott retired in 1969 and wrote a memoir about his time in the FBI, OSS and the CIA. He completed the manuscript, *It Came Too Late*, and made plans to discuss the contents of the book with CIA director, Richard Helms, in Washington on April 30, 1971. Four days before the agreed meeting Scott died of a heart attack.

Michael Scott told Dick Russell that James Angleton took away his father's manuscript. Angleton also confiscated three large cartons of files including a tape-recording of the voice of Lee Harvey Oswald. Michael Scott was also told by a CIA source that his father had not died from natural causes. Scott eventually got his father's manuscript back from the CIA. However, 150 pages were missing. Chapters 13 to 16 were deleted in their entirety. In fact, everything about his life after 1947 had been removed on grounds of national security.

Nancy Carole Tyler worked as secretary to Bobby Baker. At the time of the assassination she was living with Mary Jo Kopechne, who worked for George Smathers (she later became secretary to Robert Kennedy). According to W. Penn Jones Jr, it was Tyler and Kopechne who told Baker that John F. Kennedy planned to replace Lyndon B. Johnson as vice president. Tyler died in a plane crash, near Ocean City, Maryland, on May 10, 1965. Kopechne was later to die mysteriously in the car of Edward Kennedy on July 18, 1969.

Warren Reynolds was minding his used car lot on East Jefferson Street in Oak Cliff in Dallas, when he heard shots two blocks away. He thought it was a marital quarrel. Then he saw a man having a great difficulty tucking "a pistol or an automatic" in his belt, and running at the same time. Reynolds gave chase for a short piece being careful to keep his distance, but quickly lost sight of the fleeing man.

He didn't know it then, but he had apparently witnessed the flight of the killer (or one of the killers) of patrolman Jefferson David Tippit. Reynolds gave his name to a passing policeman and offered his cooperation. Television cameras zeroed in on him and wire services ran his story. Reynolds soon found himself at the center of the media spotlight.

Reynolds was not questioned until two months after the event. The FBI finally talked to him in January 1964. The FBI interview report said, "Reynolds was hesitant to definitely identify Oswald as the individual." Then it added, "He advised he is of the opinion Oswald is the person."

Reynolds and his family were harassed and threatened by unknown individuals. But upon giving the Warren Commission a firm identification of Oswald as being the Tippit murder fugitive, he said, "I don't think they are going to bother me any more."

Two days after Reynolds talked to the FBI, he was shot in the head. He was closing up his car lot for the night at the time. Nothing was stolen. A young man was arrested for the murder attempt. Darrell Wayne Garner had called a relative bragging that he shot Reynolds. But Garner had an alibi.

Nancy Jane Mooney, alias Betty McDonald, said Garner was in bed with her at the time he was supposed to have shot Reynolds. Nancy Jane had worked at Jack Ruby's Carousel Club. Garner was freed and quickly disappeared into obscurity.

Nancy Jane was picked up a week later for fighting with a girlfriend. She was arrested for disturbing the peace. The girlfriend was not arrested. Within hours after her arrest, Nancy Jane was dead. Police reports said she hanged herself with her toreador pants.

Harold Russell was with Warren Reynolds when the Officer Tippit shooting took place. Both men saw the Tippit killer escape. Russell was interviewed in January 1964, and said afterwards that the FBI had forced him to sign a statement that the fleeing man was Oswald.

A few months after the assassination, Russell went back to his home near David, Oklahoma. In July of 1965, Russell went to a party with a female friend. He seemingly went out of his mind at the party and started telling everyone he was going to be killed. He begged friends to hide him. Someone called the police. When the policemen arrived, one of them hit Russell on the head with his pistol. Russell was then taken to a hospital where he was pronounced dead a few hours later: cause of death was listed as "heart failure."

Hank Killam was a house painter that lived at Mrs. A.C. Johnson's rooming house at the same time Lee Harvey Oswald lived there. His wife, Wanda, once pushed cigarettes and drinks at Jack Ruby's club. Hank was a big man, over six feet and weighing over 200 lbs. After the assassination federal agents visited him repeatedly, causing him to lose one job after another.

Killam was absorbed by the assassination, even obsessed. Hours after the event, he came home, "white as a sheet." Wanda said he stayed up all night watching the television accounts of the assassination. Later he bought all the papers and clipped the stories about Kennedy's death.

Before Christmas, Killam left for Florida. Wanda confessed to the FBI where he had gone. Federal agents hounded him in Tampa where he was working selling cars at his brother-in-law's car lot. He soon lost his job.

Killam wrote his wife that he would be sending for her soon. He received a mysterious phone call on St. Patrick's Day and he left the house immediately. He was found later on a sidewalk in front of a broken window. His jugular vein was cut and he bled to death en route to the hospital.

There is no mention of Killam by the Warren Commission. A number of FBI documents on Killam relating to the assassination were withheld, along with documents prepared by the CIA. What is clear is that somebody considered Hank Killam a very important guy.

Police officer Roger D. Craig was on duty in Dallas on November 22, 1963 when he heard gunshots coming from the grassy knoll. Running to the location, he interviewed witnesses to the shooting. About 15 minutes later he saw a man running from the back door of the Texas Book Depository down the slope to Elm Street where he then got into a Nash station wagon that quickly left the scene.

Craig saw the man again in the office of Captain Will Fitz. It was the recently arrested Lee Harvey Oswald. When Craig told his story about the man being picked up by the station wagon, Oswald replied: "That station wagon belongs to Mrs. Paine, don't try to tie her into this, she had nothing to do with it."

Craig was also with Seymour Weitzman when the rifle was found on the sixth floor of the Texas Book Depository. He insisted that the rifle was a 7.65 Mauser and not a Mannlicher-Carcano.

Craig became unpopular with senior police officers in Dallas when he testified before the Warren Commission. He insisted he had seen Lee Harvey Oswald get into the station wagon 15 minutes after the shooting. Earl Warren and his team ignored this because it showed that at least two people were involved in the assassination. Craig, unlike Seymour Weitzman, refused to change his mind about finding a Mauser rather than a Mannlicher-Carcano in the Texas Book Depository. Craig was fired from the police department in 1967 after he was found to have discussed his evidence with a journalist.

In 1967 Craig went to New Orleans and was a prosecution witness at the trial of Clay Shaw. Later that year he was shot at while walking to a car park. The bullet only grazed his head.

In 1973 a car forced Craig's car off a mountain road and he was badly injured. In 1974 Craig survived another shooting in Waxahachie, Texas. The following year he was seriously wounded when his car engine suddenly exploded. Craig told friends that he was certain that the Mafia had decided to kill him. Craig was found dead from on May 15, 1975. It was later decided he had died as a result of self-inflicted gunshot wounds.

William Whaley, known as the "Oswald Cabbie," was one of the few who had the opportunity to talk alone with the accused killer. He testified that Oswald hailed him at the Dallas Greyhound bus station. Whaley said he drove Oswald to the intersection of Beckley and Neches, half a block from the rooming house where Oswald lived with his wife. Later he identified Oswald as his fare in a police line-up.

Whaley was killed in a head-on collision on a bridge over the Trinity River, December 18, 1965; his passenger was critically injured. The 83-year-old driver of the other car was also killed. Whaley had been with the City Transportation Company since 1936 and had a perfect driving record. He was the first Dallas cabbie to be killed on duty since 1937. The manager of the cab company told one Kennedy investigator: "If you're smart, you won't be coming around here asking questions."

Domingo Benavides, an auto mechanic, was witness to the murder of Officer Tippit. Benavides testified he got a "really good view of the slayer" and said the killer resembled newspaper pictures of Oswald, but he described him differently, "I remember the back of his head seemed like his hairline went square instead of tapered off . . ."

Benavides reported that he was repeatedly threatened by the police who advised him not to talk about what he saw. In mid-February 1964, Benavides brother Eddy, who looked a lot like him, was fatally shot in the back of the head at a beer joint on Second Avenue in Dallas. The case was marked "unsolved."

Benavides' father-in-law, J.W. Jackson, began his own inquiry into the shooting was shot at in his home. As the mysterious gunman escaped, a police car came around the block. It made no attempt to follow the speeding car with the gunman. The police advised that Jackson should "lay off this business and don't go around asking questions; that's our job." Jackson and Benavides are both convinced that Eddy's murder was a case of mistaken identity and that Domingo Benavides, the Tippit witness, was the intended victim.

Lee Bowers' was one of the 65 witnesses at Dealey Plaza who saw the President's assassination, and who thought shots were fired from the area of the grassy knoll. However, Bowers' was in a unique position to observe some pretty unusual activity in the Knoll area before and during the assassination. Bowers, then a towerman for the Union Terminal Co., was stationed in his 14-foot tower directly behind the grassy knoll. He faced the scene of the assassination. He could see the railroad overpass to his right. Directly in front of him was a parking lot and a wooden stockade fence, and a row of trees running along the top of the grassy knoll. The knoll sloped down to the spot on Elm Street where the President was killed. Police had "shut off" traffic into the parking lot "so that anyone moving around could actually be seen," Bowers said.

Bowers testified to the Warren Commission that he saw three unfamiliar cars slowly cruising around the parking area in the 35 minutes before the assassination; the first two left after a few minutes. The driver of the second car appeared to be talking into a "microphone or telephone;" holding something up to his mouth with one hand and he was driving with the other. A third car with out-of-state license plates and mud up to the windows, probed all around the parking area. Bowers last remembered seeing it about eight minutes before the shooting, pausing "just above the assassination site."

Bowers also observed two unfamiliar men standing on the top of the knoll at the edge of the parking lot, within 10 or 15 feet of each other. "One man, middle aged or slightly older, fairly heavy set, in a white shirt, fairly dark trousers. Another man, younger, about mid-twenties, in either a plaid shirt or plaid coat or jacket." Both were facing toward Elm and Houston in anticipation of the motorcade. The two were the only strangers he remembered seeing. His description shows a remarkable similarity to Julia Ann Mercer's description of two unidentified men climbing the knoll.

When the shots rang out, Bowers' attention was drawn to the area where he had seen the two men; he could still make out the one in the white shirt: "The darker dressed man was too hard to distinguish from the trees."

Bowers observed "some commotion at that spot . . . something out of the ordinary, a sort of milling around . . . which attracted my eye for some reason which I could not identify." At that moment, a motorcycle policeman left the Presidential motorcade and roared up the grassy knoll, straight to where the two mysterious gentlemen were standing. Later, Bowers testified that the "commotion" that caught his eye could have been a "flash of light or smoke, possibly from a gun."

On the morning of August 9, 1966, Lee Bowers, vice president of a construction firm, was driving south of Dallas on business. He was two miles south of Midlothian, Texas when his brand new company car veered from the road and hit a bridge abutment. Bowers died in a Dallas hospital, there was no autopsy and he was cremated. A doctor from Midlothian who rode to Dallas in the ambulance with Bowers noticed something peculiar about the victim. "He was in some strange sort of shock." The doctor said, "It was a different kind of shock than the accident victim experiences. I can't explain it. I've never seen anything like it."

THE STRANGE DEATH OF LIEUTENANT COMMANDER WILLIAM PITZER

Lieutenant Commander William Bruce Pitzer, who had supposedly taken photographs of Kennedy during the Presidents autopsy, was seen by a colleague,

Dennis D. David, working on a 16-mm film, slides and black and white photos of the autopsy. David noted that those materials showed what appeared to be an entry wound in the right frontal area with a corresponding exit wound in the lower rear of the skull.

Jerrol F. Custer, an X-ray technician at Bethesda, later stated that Pitzer had photographed the proceedings, including the military men who attended the Kennedy autopsy. It was also rumored that Pitzer had copies of Kennedy's autopsy photographs.

According to Dr. Joseph Humes, Pitzer was not present at the autopsy. However, he admitted that the Bethesda Naval Hospital was equipped with closed-circuit television. This was the responsibility of Pitzer and over the years had used these facilities to make instructional movies. It is therefore possible that Pitzer had secretly made a 16-mm movie film of the autopsy on President Kennedy's body, without being present in the autopsy room when it was carried out.

On October 29, 1966, Lieutenant Commander William B. Pitzer was found dead at the Naval Medical School, Bethesda. Investigations by the Naval Investigative Service and the FBI later concluded that a gunshot wound to the head had been self-inflicted.

During the weekend on which Pitzer died, the Kennedy family transferred formal possession of the materials relating to the late president's autopsy to the National Archives. An investigation carried out by Dr. Cyril H. Wecht in 1993 revealed that some items were missing. This included Kennedy's brain that had been stored in a stainless-steel container.

FBI files on the investigation, released in 1997 under the Freedom of Information Act, revealed that there was a strong possibility that Pitzer had been murdered. The paraffin tests of Pitzer's right palm and back of hand were negative, indicating the absence of nitrate, therefore no exposure to gunpowder. FBI tests indicated: "that the revolver must have been held at a distance of more than three feet when discharged."

Although there were links between Pitzer and the revolver found near the body, the FBI could find no record of Pitzer acquiring live ammunition. The autopsy showed both an entry and exit wound to the head. It also revealed a third wound that was not related to the gunshot to the head.

Pitzer had been busy writing notes to people in the time just before he was killed. However, he did not leave a suicide note. One of these notes was found on the floor near Pitzer's body. It bore a partial heel print that was not from the shoes Pitzer was wearing.

In May 1995, ex-Special Forces Colonel Daniel Marvin claimed to have been solicited by an agent of the CIA to "terminate" William Pitzer. An interview with Mavin later appeared in the sixth episode of the 1995 television series ***The Men Who Killed Kennedy***.

In his 2002 book ***The Unconventional Warrior***, Col Marvin writes:

It was early in August 1965 that I was asked by the CIA to kill U.S.
Navy Lieutenant Commander William Bruce Pitzer. Shortly after

lunch I was summoned to our headquarters where Colonel C. W. Patten told me that a 'Company man' was waiting in the nearby pine trees to meet with me. Though Colonel Patten was my commanding officer, he had no idea what it was about, familiar only with the fact our visitor was looking for a 'volunteer.'

"Its the way the 'game' is played," I thought to myself, all the while feeling the beginnings of an adrenaline surge, that shot of extra strength and endurance needed to get me through impossible situations. My mind conjured up wild thoughts about the yet unknown: what sort of intrigue might be in store for the 'volunteer' he was seeking?

Only too soon I would learn what I thought at the time to be too much. I now thank God for what I learned in that moment of truth from a CIA Operative searching for a volunteer that would open a door to unlock part of the mystery surrounding the assassination of John F. Kennedy and the untimely demise of those who would open the can of worms that surrounded the conspiracy cover-up.

Perhaps a hundred yards into the wooded area behind Group headquarters a slender man of about 5'10" waited. dressed casually in short sleeves, light slacks and sunglasses appropriate for the August heat, he flashed his ID, shook my hand and spoke to me in a low and steady voice, asking if I would terminate a man who was preparing to give States secrets to the enemy - a would-be traitor? Not only was I an overzealous patriot at the time, I was trained in assassination techniques and told that I could be asked to volunteer for such a mission outside the United States.

Performing that type of mission 'outside the US' was a crucial factor in our 'understanding.' Along with the others undergoing the same type of training, I was led to believe that the 'resources' of the Mafia were to be drawn on by the CIA via an 'arrangement' with them for the fulfillment of Stateside contracts. I was unaware of any rift that had developed between family Dons and the CIA hierarchy. I assumed the 'hit' would be overseas as I was on special orders to report to the 5th Special Forces in South Vietnam some four months hence.

Without hesitation I said "sure," thinking that once I was in Vietnam I could easily be flown via CIA owned Southern Air Transport to wherever my 'target' happened to be at that time. Once I had accomplished my mission I would return to 5th Group as arranged by the agent in charge, who would be the only one knowing where I'd been or what I'd done.

It was then told to me that it was Lieutenant Commander William Bruce Pitzer whom they wanted "taken care of" before his retirement at Bethesda Naval Hospital. I refused because it was to be done in the United States. As I left, the agent went on to meet at least one other Green Beret officer that afternoon, perhaps finding a volunteer to do his bidding: LCDR William Bruce Pitzer was found shot dead in his office on 29 October 1966, victim of an assassination conspiracy, shot down in cold blood before he could show the world what he knew about the JFK assassination.

Joyce Pitzer knew that her husband had not committed suicide. Within 24 hours of her husband's death she received a visit from an individual in Naval Intelligence who told her that she was not to talk to anyone, not even family, about the death of her husband. When Mrs. Pitzer requested the return of her husband's wedding band, she was informed that his left hand was so mutilated that removal of the ring was impossible. She never did receive it. Yet, the autopsy report states that there were no wounds on the body other than those to the head. It took Joyce Pitzer over 25 years of requests to finally get a copy of the autopsy on her husband. Colonel Daniel Marvin believes the autopsy that Joyce finally received was not that of her husband.

THE KILLINGS CONTINUE

When the Select Committee on Intelligence Activities and Select Committee on Assassinations began investigating Kennedy's death in the 1970s the deaths of potential witnesses increased dramatically. This included several criminals with links to the secret Executive Action plan to kill foreign political leaders. Those who were killed or who died in suspicious circumstances during this period included Lucien Sarti (1972), Thomas Davis (1973), Richard Cain (1973), Dave Yarras (1974), Sam Giancana (1975), Jimmy Hoffa (1975), Roland Masferrer (1975), Johnny Roselli (1976), George De Mohrenschildt (1977), Charlie Nicoletti (1977) and Carlos Prio (1977).

William Sullivan, the main figure in the FBI involved in the Executive Action project, was shot dead near his home in Sugar Hill, New Hampshire, on November 9, 1977. Sullivan had been scheduled to testify before the House Select Committee on Assassinations.

Sullivan was one of six top FBI officials who died in a six-month period in 1977. Others who were due to appear before the committee who died included Louis Nicholas, special assistant to J. Edgar Hoover and his liaison with the Warren Commission; Alan H. Belmont, special assistant to Hoover; James Cadigan, document expert with access to documents that related to death of John F. Kennedy; J. M. English, former head of FBI Forensic Sciences Laboratory where Oswald's rifle and pistol were tested and Donald Kaylor, FBI fingerprint chemist who examined prints found at the assassination scene.

Several important figures in the Central Intelligence Agency died before they could give evidence to the House Select Committee on Assassinations

Investigations. William Harvey, head of the ZR/RIFLE project, died as a result of complications from heart surgery in June 1976. William Pawley, who took part in Operation Tilt, died of gunshot wounds in January 1977. David Morales, who some believe organized the assassination, died aged 53, on May 8, 1978.

John Paisley was deputy director of the Office of Strategic Research. On September 24, 1978, John Paisley, took a trip on his motorized sailboat on Chesapeake Bay. Two days later his boat was found moored in Solomons, Maryland. Paisley's body was found in Maryland's Patuxent River. The body was tied to diving weights and he had been shot in the head. Police investigators described it as "an execution-type murder." However, officially Paisley's death was recorded as a suicide.

According to the journalist, Victor Marchetti, Paisley was a close friend of Yuri Nosenko. Marchetti also claimed that Paisley knew a great deal about the assassination of John F. Kennedy and was murdered during the House Select Committee on Assassinations investigation because he was "about to blow the whistle."

Lou Staples, a radio announcer who was doing a good many of his radio shows on the Kennedy assassination, was murdered sometime on Friday night, May 13, 1977 near Yukon, Oklahoma. He had been broadcasting radio programs on the assassination since 1973 and the response to his programs was overwhelming.

Lou's death was termed suicide, but the bullet ending his life entered behind his right temple and Lou was left-handed. Lou had been saying that he wanted to purchase some property to build a home and was lured out to a wheat field where an unknown assailant shot him.

John Roselli first became involved in organized crime when he worked for Al Capone in the 1920s. By the end of the Second World War Roselli had emerged as a senior crime boss in Las Vegas with close links to Meyer Lansky. In 1947 the FBI identified him as a leading figure in the Mafia and a close associate of Santos Trafficante.

In March 1960, President Dwight Eisenhower of the United States approved a CIA plan to overthrow Fidel Castro. The plan involved a budget of $13 million to train "a paramilitary force outside Cuba for guerrilla action." Richard Bissell and Richard Helms organized the strategy.

Sidney Gottlieb of the CIA Technical Services Division was asked to come up with proposals that would undermine Castro's popularity with the Cuban people. Plans included a scheme to spray a television studio in which he was about to appear with a hallucinogenic drug and contaminating his shoes with thallium that they believed would cause the hair in his beard to fall out.

These schemes were rejected and instead Bissell decided to arrange the assassination of Fidel Castro. In September 1960, Richard Bissell and Allen W. Dulles, the director of the CIA initiated talks with two leading figures of the Mafia, Roselli (using the name John Rawlston) and Sam Giancana.

On March 12, 1961, William Harvey arranged for CIA operative, Jim O'Connell, to meet Sam Giancana, Santo Trafficante, Johnny Roselli and Robert Maheu at the Fontainebleau Hotel. During the meeting O'Connell gave poison pills and $10,000 to Rosselli to be used against Fidel Castro. As Richard D. Mahoney points out in his book **Sons and Brothers**: "Late one evening, probably March 13, Rosselli passed the poison pills and the money to a small, reddish-haired Afro-Cuban by the name of Rafael 'Macho' Gener in the Boom Boom Room, a location Giancana thought 'stupid.' Rosselli's purpose, however, was not just to assassinate Castro, but also to set up the Mafia's partner in crime, the United States government. Accordingly, he was laying a long, bright trail of evidence that unmistakably implicated the CIA in the Castro plot. This evidence, whose purpose was blackmail, would prove critical in the CIA's cover-up of the Kennedy assassination."

In 1961 Roselli persuaded Meyer Lansky, to join the conspiracy and was reportedly offering a million-dollar reward for the Cuban leader's murder. Roselli also recruited Richard Cain, a specialist in electronics and wiretaps. Cain took part in a failed attempt in March 1961 to poison Castro.

The nearest Rosselli came to killing Fidel Castro was in September 1961. Several Cubans were arrested at the intersection of Rancho Boyeros Avenue and Santa Catalina Avenue in Havana. The men were in two Jeeps armed with bazookas, grenade launchers, and machine guns. Two of those arrested, Guillermo Caula Ferrer and Higinio Menendez, made a full confession during their interrogation and admitted they had been working with CIA agents in Miami and had been trained on Guantanamo, the American naval base in Cuba. All the men involved in the plot were executed.

In April 1962, William Harvey took control of the ZR/RIFLE project. He told Johnny Roselli that Santos Trafficante and Sam Giancana had to cease involvement in the project to kill Castro. Ted Shackley, the new head of JM WAVE, also began to play a more important role in planning the assassination.

Eventually Rosselli and his friends became convinced that simply removing its leader could not reverse the Cuban revolution. However, they continued to play along with this CIA plot in order to prevent them being prosecuted for criminal offences committed in the United States.

In February 1963, William Harvey was removed as head of the ZR/RIFLE project. Harvey was now sent to Italy where he became Chief of Station in Rome. Harvey was convinced that Robert Kennedy had been responsible for his demotion. A friend of Harvey's said that he "hated Bobby Kennedy's guts with a purple passion."

Harvey continued to keep in contact with Johnny Roselli. According to Richard D. Mahoney: "On April 8, Rossrlli flew to New York to meet with Bill Harvey. A week later, the two men met again in Miami to discuss the plot in greater detail."

On April 21, Harvey flew from Washington to deliver four poison pills directly to Rosselli, who got them to Tony Varona and hence to Havana. That same evening, Harvey and Ted Shackley, the chief of the CIA's south Florida base, drove a U-Haul truck filled with the requested arms through the rain to a deserted parking lot in Miami. They got out and handed the keys to Rosselli. In November 1963, Roselli traveled to Arizona with a male friend and two women. The FBI was following him but on the way to Los Vegas they lost contact with him. According to Tosh Plumlee, a pilot working for the CIA, he picked up Roselli from Tampa, Florida, early on the 22nd November. Plumlee then took Roselli to New Orleans.

After picking up three more men, Plumlee took Roselli and his friends to Redbird Airport in Dallas. In an interview in April 1992, Plumlee claimed that he was told that the objective was "to abort the assassination" of John F. Kennedy.

Roselli discovered in 1966 that the FBI had been collecting information on his activities. Attempts were made to deport him as an illegal alien. Roselli moved to Los Angeles where he went into early retirement. It was at this time he told attorney, Edward Morgan: "The last of the sniper teams dispatched by Robert Kennedy in 1963 to assassinate Fidel Castro were captured in Havana. Under torture they broke and confessed to being sponsored by the CIA and the US government. At that point, Castro remarked that, 'If that was the way President Kennedy wanted it, Cuba could engage in the same tactics.' The result was that Castro infiltrated teams of snipers into the U.S. to kill Kennedy."

Morgan took the story to Jack Anderson and drew Pearson. The story was then passed on to Earl Warren. He did not want anything to do with it and so the information was then passed to the FBI. When they failed to investigate the story Anderson wrote an article entitled "President Johnson is sitting on a political H-bomb" about Roselli's story. It has been suggested that Roselli started this story at the request of his friends in the Central Intelligence Agency in order to divert attention from the investigation being carried out by Jim Garrison.

Roselli was eventually charged with being involved in illegal gambling in Las Vegas. In an attempt to obtain a lenient sentence, Roselli provided information in court about his role in helping the CIA with Operation Mongoose and ZR/RIFLE. The judge was not impressed and he was sent to McNeal Island prison. His good friend Fred Black intervened and used his powerful political connections to get transferred to a less harsh prison. Roselli was eventually released in 1973.

In 1975 Frank Church and his Select Committee on Intelligence Activities interviewed Roselli about his relationship with the secret services. It emerged from this interview that Roselli and fellow crime boss, Sam Giancana had taken part in talks with the CIA about the possibility of murdering Fidel Castro. Roselli also claimed that a CIA hit team that had been dispatched to Cuba had been "turned" and used to kill Kennedy.

The following year the Select Committee on Intelligence Activities decided to recall Roselli. Soon afterwards Fred Black called him and warned him that Santos Trafficante had taken out a contract on his life and that the "Cubans were after him."

In July 1976, Roselli left home in Florida to play golf. He never arrived at the golf course and ten days later his body was found floating in an oil drum in Miami's Dumfoundling Bay. He had been garroted. Roselli's legs had been sawed off and squashed into the drum with the rest of his body.

Jack Anderson, of the *Washington Post*, interviewed Roselli just before he was murdered. On September 7 1976, the newspaper reported Roselli as saying: "When Oswald was picked up, the underworld conspirators feared he would crack and disclose information that might lead to them. This almost certainly would have brought a massive U.S. crackdown on the Mafia. So Jack Ruby was ordered to eliminate Oswald."

The House Select Committee on Assassinations managed to obtain the records of an FBI wiretap on Santos Trafficante. On the tape Trafficante was heard to say: "now only two people know who killed Kennedy and they aren't talking."

In an interview in April 1992, Tosh Plumlee claimed that Roselli had been killed because he knew too much about Operation Mongoose and the assassination of President Kennedy.

It is very clear that the large majority of these murders eliminated witnesses to, participants in, or investigators of the Kennedy assassination. Unfortunately, the death list does not end here. The murders of Robert Kennedy, Martin Luther King, and the attempted assassinations of George Wallace and President Gerald Ford, all seem to have their list of suspicious deaths surrounding those who were involved in one way or another.

The evidence is overwhelming that the deaths of President Kennedy and others was not the act of crazed "lone gunmen," but a conspiracy of many, possibly fascist elements entrenched in the United States government, military and intelligence. Assassination is an effective tool. Not only murder en-mass, but the individual death of those that could make a difference, the politicians that might make a change, and the people that stood in the way.

Assassination has been a long-term technique for certain political purposes; and it is time that the public wakes up and takes notice to what is going on around them. Because they are killing us; not only are they killing people at the top government levels, but all the way down to the activists and those who are trying to make a difference.

President Kennedy shortly before he was shot in Dallas.

CHAPTER THREE
A Deadly Pursuit

For a number of investigators, research into the mysteries of the UFO phenomenon can be as hazardous as investigating the JFK assassination. For something that the Air Force says does not exist and poses no threat to national security, there has been an extraordinary amount of effort over the years to dissuade researchers from pursuing the phenomenon too deeply.

Much has been written about UFO investigators who have been threatened with bodily harm if they do not give up their UFO research. Dennis Balthaser, a UFO researcher and former investigator for the International UFO Museum in Roswell, New Mexico, had just such an experience in 1997 when the Roswell museum received a phone call from a man in Stillwater, Oklahoma, claiming to be the son of a former military policeman who was on hand in 1947 to witness the Roswell Incident, a famous, alleged UFO crash. The man said his father has seen one live and three dead aliens and had a piece of strange metal from the crash site. The man agreed to meet with Balthaser.

But when Balthaser arrived at the appointed site, a Denny's restaurant in Stillwater, he was met by a man and a woman who told him, "We are not who you were expecting." They said they were from the Air Force Office of Special Investigations. The agents told him his home and museum phones had been tapped. He felt intimidated, if not directly threatened.

"I was scared," he said.

It is frightening enough to consider that the military could be closely watching your activity, add to that the fear of the unknown when mysterious strangers dressed in black start knocking on your front door in the middle of the night. In the weird world of UFOs, the Men-In-Black (MIB) seems to represent the devil made flesh. Mysterious men who arrive to warn, harass, even threaten UFO experiencers and researchers into silence. Stories of the MIB have become ingrained in UFO folklore to such an extent that they have become archetypical symbols of the dark side of UFOlogy.

To those who have actually been unfortunate enough to receive a visit from the MIB, the event is usually so unusual and frightening that the reality of the experience cannot be questioned. Again we are left with stories that seem to transcend our normal reality and ventures into a strange world populated by aliens, ghosts, monsters and other strange creatures that are very real to those who happen to meet up with them.

A BRIEF HISTORY OF THE MEN-IN-BLACK

In the broadest terms, the Men-In-Black are said to be involved in the silencing of UFO witnesses and investigators. They are usually described as the three Men-In-Black, but this tends to be an over-generalization as these mysterious strangers are just as often seen in pairs or even lone individuals. Strangely enough, there have also been a few reports of female "MIB." There seems to be no sexual discrimination when it comes to scaring UFO researchers.

A tradition of mysterious dark-clothed individuals with sinister intentions can be traced back to ancient times and across any culture. As far back as biblical times, and possibly even further back, there has been a tradition in the Middle East of men in black robes attempting to lure victims out into the desert for sinister purposes. Furthermore, in Europe during the middle ages there existed a fear in rural areas of black-clad beings that preyed on the blood of humans and livestock alike.

Fairy myths and lore often speak of human-looking fairies that dress in black and cause mischief in the human world. The fact that MIB are often described as having Asian features is interesting in light of the fact that there is a long-standing myth in China, Tibet, and India that a superior race of humans live beneath the surface of the earth who occasionally send "agents" dressed in black to the surface to check out and manipulate human affairs. Native Americans feared the "Black Man" or "Trickster" who supposedly lurked in the dark, wild forests of North America.

Why these strange beings have crossed over into the bizarre world of UFOs is a mystery known only to them, and they're not talking.

The modern mythos around UFOs and the MIB can be traced to former UFO researcher Albert K. Bender, founder of the International Flying Saucer Bureau. In September 1953 Bender had received information that he felt offered a good explanation concerning the origin of flying saucers. Bender wrote down his theory and sent it off to a friend he felt he could trust. When the three men appeared at Benders door, one of them held that letter in his hand.

The three men told Bender that among the many saucer researchers he had been the one to stumble upon the correct answer to the flying saucer enigma. Then they filled him in on the details. Bender became ill. He was unable to eat for three days.

"They were pretty rough with me," Bender later wrote. "Two men did all the talking and the other kept watching me all the time they were here. He didn't take his eyes off me."

Bender went on to say that when people found out the truth about flying saucers there would be dramatic changes in all things. Science especially would suffer a major blow. Political structures would topple. Mass confusion would reign. Allegedly because of his unsettling experience, Bender stopped investigating UFO reports, moved away and started a new life. The UFO Silencers had struck. It wouldn't be their last appearance. Even though Albert Benders experience served as the platform to launch the modern era of MIB encounters, there are accounts of past incidents that seem to be the early precursors of the MIB.

In 1864 a UFO dropped several chunks of metal over a small Texas community. The metal was retrieved and placed in a store window on the main street of town. The very next day a "stranger" dressed in a long black coat visited the shopkeeper and offered a fair amount of cash for the objects. The shopkeeper, who didn't own the objects, refused to sell. That night the store caught fire and when the ashes and rubble were sifted through, none of the artifacts could be found, and the "stranger" was never seen again.

A WORLD WIDE PHENOMENON

Skeptics are fond of saying that MIB reports are probably nothing more than folklore and copycat hoaxes gleaned from books and magazines. However, the MIB have not confined themselves to the U.S. alone as was discovered by one Chinese UFO investigator.

Author Shi Bo revealed in his 1983 book ***China and Extraterrestrials*** that in May 1963, after spotting "a shining, silvery disc" hanging in the sky of Yangguan, Shansi province, six-year-old Li Jing-yang was stopped in the street by "a very tall man dressed entirely in black."

The man, while pointing to the exact spot where Li had seen the disc, inquired as to whether the boy had seen anything unusual in the sky recently. Li responded that indeed he had, which elicited a warning from the man to "never tell anyone else" what he had seen.

The MIB then went around a corner and seemingly disappeared. Li claims that this encounter was witnessed by several others who all noted and discussed the stranger's odd, mechanical movements, his automated-sounding voice, and the fact that his lips did not move when he spoke.

The one consistent thing you can say about the MIB is that they are entirely inconsistent. You don't even have to have a UFO sighting to be visited by one of these strange beings.

Peter Rojcewicz, a professor of humanities and folklore at New York's Juilliard School, had an unexpected encounter in 1980 in the University of Pennsylvania library. Rojcewict remembers that he was just reading a UFO book suggested by another professor when he noticed standing in front of him a "very gaunt, very pale man."

"He was about 6 foot tall and weighed about 140 pounds and wore a black suit, black shoes, black string tie and a bright white shirt," Rojcewicz said. "His suit was loose and it looked as though he had slept in it for three days."

The strange man sat down like he had dropped from the ceiling, "all in one movement" and folded his hands on top of a stack of books in front of him. The Man in Black asked Rojcewicz what he was doing. Rojcewicz said he was reading about flying saucers.

"Have you seen a flying saucer?" the Man in Black asked. Rojcewicz said he hadn't.

"Do you believe in the reality of flying saucers?"

Rojcewicz said he didn't know much about them and wasn't sure he was very interested in the phenomena.

The man screamed: "Flying saucers are the most important fact of the century and you are not interested?"

"I tried to calm him," Rojcewicz said. But the man quickly got up, once again all in a single awkward movement, put his hand on Rojcewicz's shoulder and said: "Go well on your purpose" and left.

"In 10 seconds I was overwhelmed by fear...I had a sense that this man was out of the ordinary and that idea frightened me...I got up and walked around the stacks toward where the reference librarians usually are. The librarians weren't there. There were no guards, in fact there was nobody else in the library..I was terrified."

Rojcewicz went back to the table where he had been reading: "to get myself together. It took me about an hour. Then I got up and everything was back to normal, the people were all there."

These kinds of experiences are far from unique, with UFO researchers files bulging with similar reports. Although these accounts can vary to a strong degree, there are enough to suggest an underlying pattern.

NO EASY ANSWERS

Many UFO investigators believe that the MIB are actually working for government agencies, and that they are threatening UFO witnesses into silence. They are perhaps helping to conceal some kind of special military or intelligence operation. One major drawback to this theory is that there have been no reports where these mysterious figures have actually carried out their threats. Something quite puzzling when you think of the vast number of UFO/Alien encounters that over the years have become public knowledge.

Much like the UFO mystery, the MIB could be several different situations that bear superficial resemblance to each other. Some MIB could very well be humans from secret military or government groups. Others could be extraterrestrials disguised, as best they can, to look human. Others seem to be more closely related to supernatural beings that have dwelled on the outskirts of the human mind since the beginning of time.

There is probably no easy explanation on why these strange beings occasionally take on the role of UFO silencers. Perhaps the simple spreading of fear and confusion, and not the more complex silencing of UFO witnesses, is the ultimate goal of these mysterious strangers from the dark side. However, there is a more sinister side to the silencing of UFO witnesses and researchers.

In an article called: ***Other Mysterious Deaths: Lest We Forget***, published in 1997 in ***UFO Universe*** magazine, Prof. G. Cope Schellhorn writes that the recent suspicious deaths of UFO investigators only seem to add emphasis to a reality with which many of the more aware UFOlogists are now quite familiar: not only is UFO research potentially dangerous, but the life span of the average serious investigator falls far short of the national average.

Mysterious and suspicious deaths among UFO investigators are nothing new. In 1971, the well-known author and researcher Otto Binder wrote an article for ***Saga*** magazine's ***Special UFO Report*** titled: ***Liquidation of the UFO Investigators***. Binder had researched the deaths of "no less than 137 flying saucer researchers, writers, scientists, and witnesses' who had died in the previous 10 years, "many under the most mysterious circumstances."

The selected cases Binder offered were loaded with a plethora of alleged heart attacks, suspicious cancers and what appears to be outright examples of murder. We will have occasion to refer to many of these cases, but first let us take a look at more recent evidence of highly suspect deaths among present day researchers.

One disturbing case is the death of Ron Rummel, ex-Air Force intelligence agent and publisher of the *Alien Digest*, on August 6, 1993. Rummel allegedly shot himself in the mouth with a pistol. Friends say, however, that no blood was found on the pistol barrel and the handle of the weapon was free of fingerprints. Also, according to information now circulating, a left-handed person wrote the suicide note left by the deceased. Rummel was right-handed. Perspiration on the body smelled like sodium pentothal, or so it is alleged.

The Alien Digest ran to seven limited issues, all now almost impossible to acquire. One thing is certain. Ron Rummel's magazine was touching on sensitive issues such as the predator/prey aspect of the alien/human relationship and the use of humans as food and recyclable body parts. Did Rummel cross a forbidden line? It would seem so. But which line, and where?

Ron Johnson

An equally disturbing death is that of Ron (Jerrold) Johnson, at the time MUFON's Deputy Director of Investigations. Johnson was 43 years old and, it would seem, in excellent health. He had just passed a recent physical examination with the proverbial flying colors. However, on June 9, 1994, while attending a Society of Scientific Exploration meeting in Austin, Texas, Johnson died quickly and amid very strange circumstances. During a slide show, several people sitting close to him heard a gasp. When the lights were turned back on, Johnson was slumped over in his chair, his face purple, blood oozing from his nose. A soda can, from which he had been sipping, was sitting on the chair next to him.

Did Ron Johnson die of a stroke, or possibly an allergic reaction? Some of the more outstanding facts of Ron Johnson's life might easily lead a more skeptical-minded person to a tentative conclusion that his death was probably neither accidental nor natural. For instance, his most recent job was with the Institute of Advanced Studies, purportedly working on UFO propulsion systems.

Johnson had been formerly employed by Earth Tech, Inc., a private Austin, Texas think tank headed by Harold Puthoff. It would appear he held high security clearances, traveled frequently between San Antonio and White Sands, and had attended two secret NATO meetings in the last year or so.

One of those meetings, it is rumored dealt with ET communications. Although advanced in years, there are some who believe that Dr. Hynek's death was because of "strange circumstances," due to the high number of researchers who have died of brain tumors or cancer. If all or most of the facts offered above are accurate, one thing seems obvious: Johnson was walking both sides of the street. This in itself was highly dangerous, and he may have paid the ultimate price in an attempt to serve more than one master.

As for exactly what killed Ron Johnson, a number of possibilities beyond natural ones present themselves. It is quite easy in this day and age to induce strokes through chemicals or pulsed radiation. It is just as easy, and has been for some time, to induce heart attacks and other physical debilitations, such as fast-acting cancers. The best bet is that a quick-acting toxin, perhaps a nerve agent, eliminated Ron Johnson. As for exactly why he was killed, we will probably never know. The autopsy, somewhat ludicrously, has been officially classified as inconclusive.

As a side note, a nurse returning home from Austin shortly after Johnson's death reported a similar death-situation aboard her plane. When she tried to move rearward to offer her assistance, she was forcefully restrained from doing so. Could it be, one wonders, that some agent, through an accident, was the victim of his own machinations? The idea strikes a nice note of poetic justice, if in fact that were the scenario.

Ann Livingston

Another death involving elements of high strangeness is that of Ann Livingston, who died in early 1994 of a fast-form of ovarian cancer. Livingston made her living as an accountant, but she was also a MUFON investigator and had in fact, published an article entitled ***Electronic Harassment and Alien Abductions*** in the November 1993 ***MUFON Journal***.

The article was highly critical of Julianne McKinney, director of the Electronic Surveillance Project of the Association of National Security Alumni. McKinney discounts UFO phenomena, believing that what passes for such is most often one kind of governmental ploy or another, whether in the form of experimental machinery or experimental psychology.

Some facts that seem relevant to the case stand out. At 7:15 AM, December 29th 1992, Livingston's apartment, close to O'Hare airport in Chicago, Illinois, was lit up brightly by a strange silver white flash. She was accosted later in the day while in her apartment parking lot by five Men-in-Black which she described as being almost faceless and carrying long, flashlight-like black objects. She was rendered unconscious.

It is not a well-known fact that Ann Livingston had been previously abducted. Her friend, Fran Heiser, has stated that Ann Livingston had met two handsome people, a man and woman, on an earlier trip to Mexico. To Livingston's surprise, the man told her that the attractive young lady she was meeting was in fact her daughter.

Karla Turner

Could genital intrusions from past UFO abductions have poisoned in some way Ann Livingston's system? That is exactly the suspicion Karla Turner (author of ***Masquerade of Angels***, ***Taken***, and ***Into the Fringe***) had about the breast cancer that preceded her death during the summer of 1996.

Both publicly and privately, Karla Turner held up the specter of alien retaliation for statements she made in print, especially in ***Masquerade of Angels***. How much her suspicions were founded in reality we will probably never know.

Who or what is killing UFO investigators now and in the past? Probably some of the deaths presented here that look at first glance so suspicious, are in fact natural or accidental or self-inflicted because of stress or mental imbalances. But, as Otto Binder noted more than 25 years ago, there are so many. Pure common sense, and good logic, should lead us to believe that the high incidence of premature death in a field that has a limited number of investigators is very disproportionate compared to the population at large.

What we may have is a spider web of interweaving threads which are causal and often, in fact, deadly. One thread is the activities of the U.S. (and other) intelligence agencies. Another thread is possible ET involvement. A third thread is the involvement of certain PSI-tech think tanks and private PSI/PK practitioners, including negative occultists.

A possible fourth thread is highly reactionary religious cults that feel they are carrying out the will of God. It is more than likely that one or more or all of the above agencies are responsible in whole or in part for many of the strange deaths that have befallen those who have been caught up in the weird world of UFOs.

THE MYSTERIOUS DEATH OF A UFO WHISTLE-BLOWER

Al Pratt suspected something was wrong with his friend Philip Schneider. For several days in a row, Al had gone to Phil's apartment, in Willsonville, Oregon, saw his car in the parking lot, but received no answer at the door.

Finally, on January 17th, 1996, Al Pratt, along with the manager of the Autumn Park Apartments and a detective from the Clackamas County Sheriff's office entered the apartment. Inside, they found the body of Philip Schneider. Apparently he had been dead for five to seven days. The Clackamas County Coroner's office initially attributed Philip Schneider's death to a stroke. However, in the following days disturbing details about his death began to surface, leading some to believe that Philip Schneider had not died from a stroke, but had in fact been murdered.

Philip Schneider's life was certainly as controversial as his death. He was born on April 23, 1947 at Bethesda Navy Hospital. Philip's parents were Oscar and Sally Schneider. Oscar Schneider was a Captain in the United States Navy, worked in nuclear medicine and helped design the first nuclear submarines. Captain Schneider was also part of OPERATION CROSSROADS, which was responsible for the testing of nuclear weapons in the Pacific at Bikini Island.

In a lecture videotaped in May 1996, Philip Schneider claimed that his father, Captain Oscar Schneider, was also involved with the infamous "Philadelphia Experiment." In addition, Philip claimed to be an ex-government structural engineer who was involved in building underground military bases (DUMB) around the country, and to be one of only three people to survive the 1979 incident between the alien Grays and U.S. military forces at the Dulce underground base. Philip Schneider's ex-wife, Cynthia drayer believes that Philip was murdered because he publicly revealed the truth about the U.S. government's involvement with UFOs.

For two years prior to his death, Philip Schneider had been on a lecture tour talking about government cover-ups, black budgets, and UFOs. Philip stated in his lecture that in 1954, under the Eisenhower administration, the federal government decided to circumvent the Constitution and form a treaty with extraterrestrials. The treaty was called the 1954 Greada Treaty.

Officials agreed that for extraterrestrial technology, the Grays could test their implanting techniques on select citizens. However, the extraterrestrials had to inform the government just who had been abducted and subject to implants. Slowly over time, the aliens altered the bargain, abducting and implanting thousands of people without reporting back to the government.

In 1979, Morrison-Knudsen, Inc employed Schneider and he was involved in building an addition to the deep underground military base at Dulce, New Mexico. The project at that time had drilled four holes in the desert that were to be linked together with tunnels.

Philip's job was to go down the holes, check the rock samples, and recommend the explosives to deal with the particular rock. In the process, the workers accidentally opened a large artificial cavern, a secret base for the aliens known as Grays.

In the panic that occurred, sixty-seven workers and military personnel were killed, with Philip Schneider being one of only three people to survive. Philip claimed that scars on his chest were caused by his being struck by an alien weapon that would later result in cancer due to the radiation.

If Philip Schneider's claims are true, then his knowledge of the secret government, UFOs and other information kept from the public, could have serious repercussions to the world, as we know it. In his lectures, Philip spoke on such topics as the Space-Defense-Initiative, black helicopters, railroad cars built with shackles to contain political prisoners, the World Trade Center bombing, and the secret black budget.

Quotes taken from a lecture given by Philip Schneider in May 1995, at Post Falls, Idaho.

RAILROAD CARS

Recently, I knew someone who lived near where I live in Portland, Oregon. He worked at Gunderson Steel Fabrication, where they make railroad cars. Now, I knew this fellow for the better part of 30 years, and he was kind of a quiet type. He came in to see me one day excited, and he told me 'they're building prisoner cars.' He was nervous. Gunderson, he said, had a contract with the federal government to build 107,200 full-length railroad cars, each with 143 pairs of shackles to hold prisoners down and against the walls. There are 11 sub-contractors in this giant project. Supposedly, Gunderson got over 2 billion dollars for the contract. Bethlehem Steel and other steel outfits are involved. He showed me one of the cars in the rail yards in North Portland. He was right. If you multiply 107,200 times 143 times 11, you come up with about 15,000,000. This is probably the number of people who disagree with the federal government.

"STAR WARS" AND THE ALIEN THREAT

68% of the military budget is directly or indirectly affected by the black budget. "Star Wars" relies heavily upon stealth weaponry. By the way, none of the stealth program would have been available if we had not taken apart crashed alien disks. None of it. Some of you might ask what the space shuttle is 'shuttling." Large ingots of special metals that are milled in space and cannot be produced on the surface of the Earth. They need the near vacuum of outer space to produce them. We are not even being told anything close to the truth. I believe our government officials have sold us down the drain - lock, stock and barrel. Up until several weeks ago, I was employed by the U.S. government with a Rhyolite-38 clearance factor - one of the highest in the world. I believe the "Star Wars" program is there solely to act as a buffer to prevent alien attack - it has nothing to do with the 'cold war,' which was only a toy to garner money from all the people. For what? The whole lie was planed and executed for the last 75 years.

BLACK HELICOPTERS

There are over 64,000 black helicopters in the United States. For every hour that goes by, there is one being built. Is this the proper use of our money? What does the federal government need 64,000 tactical helicopters for, if they are not trying to enslave us. I doubt if the entire military needs 64,000 worldwide. There are 157 F-117A stealth aircraft loaded with LIDAR and computer-enhanced imaging radar. They can see you walking from room to room when they fly over your house. They see objects in the house from the air with a variation limit of one inch to 30,000 miles. That's how accurate that is. I worked in the federal government for a long time, and I know exactly how they handle their business.

TERRORIST BOMBINGS

"I was hired not too long ago to do a report on the World Trade Center Bombing. I was hired because I know about the 90 some odd varieties of chemical explosives. I looked at the pictures taken right after the blast. The concrete was puddled and melted. The steel and the rebar were literally extruded up to six-feet longer than its original length. There is only one weapon that can do that — a small nuclear weapon. A construction-type nuclear device. Obviously, when they say that it was a nitrate explosive that did the damage, they're lying 100 percent folks. I want to further mention that with the last explosion in Oklahoma City, they are saying that it was a nitrate or fertilizer bomb that did it. " First, they came out and said it was a 1,000 pound fertilizer bomb. Then, it was 1,500, then, 2,000 pounds. Now its 20,000. You can't put 20,000 pounds of fertilizer in a Rider Truck. Now, I've never mixed explosives, per se. I know the chemical structure and the application of construction explosives. My reputation was based on it. I helped hollow out more than 13 deep underground military bases in the United States. I worked on the Malta project in West Germany, in Spain and in Italy. I can tell you from experience that a nitrate explosion would have hardly shattered the windows of the federal building in Oklahoma City. It would have killed a few people and knocked part of the facing off the building, but it would have never have done that kind of damage. I believe I have been lied to, and I am not taking it any longer, so I'm telling you that I have been lied to.

In 1987 Philip married Cynthia Marie Drayer Simon. The two had met in June of 1986 at a meeting of the Oregon Agate and Mineral Society. As Cynthia put it years later, "He had so many interesting stories, so much information to share, we bonded and love began to bloom."

Philip and Cynthia would later have a daughter, Marie Schneider. Unfortunately their marriage had difficulties. According to Cynthia, health problems contributed to their break up. Philip had multiple health concerns, many of which could have killed him. He had chronic lower back pain that never went away, even after a back operation. He had multiple Sclerosis, which was chronic and progressive. Occasionally he had to use, crutches, a body brace, leg braces, bladder bag, catheter, diapers, and a wheelchair. He often had to sleep in a hospital bed with railings, a helmet, and body braces. When Cynthia first met him he was taking Dilantin for seizures, and almost died three times from this medication due to an allergic reaction.

Philip also had Brittle Bone Syndrome (osteoporosis) and cancer in his arms. He had hundreds of shrapnel wounds, a plate in his head with a metal fragment in his brain, fingers missing from his left hand. There was a scar that ran down from the top of his throat to below his belly button, and another scar that ran from just under his ribs, side to side.

Cynthia would later state: "Philip was a complex person. He had brain damage after a bomb was dropped on him while working as a civilian structural engineer for Morrison-Knudsen in Vietnam. He had a Rhyolite clearance. He was learning disabled, brilliant in some areas, yet unable to fill out a form in the Doctors office. Able to create time travel formulas, but unable to budget money; he had to file bankruptcy one year. I now believe that he had been 'deprogrammed' so that he could not remember most of his 'past' life. But something began to happen shortly after we first met. Perhaps because of the seizures, or because he changed his medication, or because he now had another person to talk to that was interested in what he had to say, he began to remember the old days. Being the scientific, logical minded person I am, I listened intently to his stories with a grain of salt, waiting for additional information to verify them. I can still remember the night he began to talk in some foreign language (sounded like Chinese and another night in what sounded like French.) Philip told me he knew 11 languages before the brain damage. After the space shuttle, Challenger, exploded, I visited Philip in his apartment. He had a large chalk board with complicated formulas which proved that a 'Cosmosphere' had shot down the space shuttle."

Cynthia also said, "It was a difficult marriage for both of us, which was complicated by a failed self-employed business selling rocks, minerals, and antiques, Philip's re-constructive surgery on scars on his chest, his lower back operation, my gall-bladder surgery and the birth of our daughter, all within a 1 year period. The pressures of our new family, failed business, and physical problems culminated in our divorce in 1990. Philip was an emotional abuser and could be very mean and abusive. He was a complex person - part genius and part paranoid schizophrenic. We had a bad marriage but developed it into a great friendship."

One of Philip's more amazing stories was his fathers alleged involvement with the "Philadelphia Experiment." When Philip's father, Captain Oscar Schneider (Navy Medical Corp.) died in 1993, Philip discovered original letters in his basement.

According to Philip, the letters were evidence that the Philadelphia Experiment actually existed, and that Oscar Schneider had been a participant in it after the crewmembers had been quarantined in a Virginia psychiatric ward. Captain Schneider supposedly autopsied the bodies of the crew members as they died, and found alien implants in their arms, legs, behind their eyes, and deep inside their brains.

Captain Schneider was confused by these implants, so they obviously were not military. They had to have been alien in nature, and the small "transistor" like item was discovered before transistors had been invented. Here was evidence that either by accident, or on purpose, aliens were involved with the Philadelphia Experiment, and were probably responsible for its failure.

Also discovered in Oscar's basement were photographs taken during Operation Crossroads, in which a nuclear device was used on Bikini Island. Authentic military photos taken from an airplane showed UFOs raising up from the lagoon and flying through the mushroom cloud. These photos however, mysteriously disappeared from Philips apartment at the time of his death.

Some investigators in Philip Schneider's mysterious death have had problems believing some of the incredible claims he made before he died. Even those who knew Philip when he was alive didn't always accept the validity of his stories. Cynthia Schneider noted that when Philip was under crisis or pressure, he would tell people that he had been arrested, or that people from the sheriff's office or government had been at his door. This was the way he expressed his crisis. Unfortunately she claims, sometimes it was true, like "the little boy who cried wolf," his friends became numb to his reports.

Despite the fact that Philip's claims seemed too wild or disturbing to be true, he obviously believed in what he was saying. Philip claimed that his life was in danger because he was revealing the truth, a truth that some would kill to keep secret. He borrowed a gun from his friend Ron Utella, stating that he felt he needed protection and that there had been several attempts to have his car run off the road. In the end, though, Philip's safeguards were not enough to save his life. On either January 10 or 11, 1996, Philip Schneider died under mysterious circumstances.

After the initial cause of Philip's death was listed as a stroke, Cynthia asked to see the body before it was to be prepared for cremation. The funeral director who felt that the body's advanced state of decomposition would be too traumatic dissuaded her. However, she could not shake the feeling that something was wrong.

The next day Cynthia was contacted by Detective Randy Harris who said that "something was wrong" – that there were marks on Philip's neck. Philip Schneider's body was removed from the funeral home and autopsied by Dr. Karen Gunson, Medical Examiner for Multnomah County, Oregon. The autopsy revealed that Philip had in fact died as a result of having a rubber hose wrapped three times, tightly around his neck and tied in a knot. The conclusion from the autopsy was that he had committed suicide. He had wrapped the tubing around his neck, tied it in a knot, blocked the flow of blood to his head, became unconscious and finally died.

More surprising was Cynthia's discovery that Philips lecture material, unknown metals, military photographs, and all notes for his unwritten book on UFOs were missing from his apartment. However, money and other valuables were left untouched.

When he was found in his apartment, Philip's body was in an unusual position. His feet were under the bed, his head was in a wheelchair seat, at an unusual angle, and the rest of his body was on the floor, hands by his sides. There was blood found on the floor near the wheelchair, but no blood was found on the wheelchair. There were no apparent wounds on Philip's body to account for the blood.

No sample of the blood was taken due to the initial belief that Philip had died of natural causes. No suicide note has ever been found. In fact, Mark Rufener, a long time friend of Philip said, "I saw Philip the weekend of January 6 and 7th 1996. We were going to buy land in Colorado. We were excited because he was going to hire me to help write a book about his knowledge on UFOs and aliens, the One World Government, and the Black Budget. He did not commit suicide, he was murdered and it was made to look like a suicide."

When he was alive, Philip enjoyed eating out at the 76 Truck Stop in Aurora, Oregon. A waitress named Donna remembered his stops when they would talk about his work. Philip mentioned to her that there had been 19 attempts to stop him from talking. Donna states that Philip said: "If they ever say that I have committed suicide, you will know that I have been murdered." She said that Philip believed he had a mission to talk about a government cover-up about aliens and UFOs, and that there were force's out to stop people who talked.

Was Philip Schneider murdered? His ex-wife Cynthia believes this to be the case. She thinks that someone met Philip he knew and injected with a drug in order TO incapacitate him. The assailants then wrapped the rubber hose around his neck, asphyxiating him. In fact, shortly after Philip's death, several friends told Cynthia that they had seen Philip with an unknown blond woman several weeks before he died.

During the course of the meeting, Cynthia noticed a longhaired blond woman in a car, watching the meeting through the window with a pair of binoculars. When they tried to approach the car, the woman quickly sped away. Cynthia later traced the license plate number and it turned out to be from a truck, with the plate reported as stolen. Cynthia thinks the reports of women with blond hair is significant because Cynthia's mother, through a channeling session, had told her that a woman wearing a blond wig was involved in Philip's death.

Despite the fact that officials have closed the case as a suicide, and Philip's surviving siblings have tried to persuade Cynthia to accept the ruling, Cynthia has not stopped in her efforts to discover the truth in her ex-husband's death. She says that she knows in her heart and soul that Philip would not have committed suicide willingly, and she still hopes that Philips blood and urine can be relocated by the Multnomah County Medical Examiner's Office and examined for traces of drugs that would not normally be there.

However, as the days go by the reality for such tests grows smaller. She still hopes that someone will come forward with pertinent information to help her find justice for Philip's death. Until that time comes, Cynthia drayer will continue her task, perhaps putting her own safety at risk. That prospect doesn't frighten her anymore, "I just want people to know the truth about Philip Schneider, a person who died trying to expose the difficult truths of this world."

THE DANGERS OF UFO INVESTIGATION

Certainly neither the public at large and not even UFOlogists generally seem thoroughly aware of the real risks UFO investigators run. In fact those UFOlogists who are aware of the suspicious deaths of some of their colleagues in the 50s and 60s, seem to believe that whatever forces and agencies that were then responsible have softened their tactics.

The evidence, as we have indicated, does not seem to support such a conclusion. There is no doubt, however, that the `50s and `60s produced some strange goings-on.

Undoubtedly, the most intriguing (and perhaps appalling) deaths in UFOlogy were those of Dorothy Kilgallen, M.K. Jessup and Dr. James McDonald, the former an alleged accident, the latter two purported suicides.

The details of these deaths, despite official pronouncements to the contrary, are disturbing to say the least. Each of the three individuals seemed to have much to live for, all were successful, and every one of them was deeply immersed in the relatively new UFO-phenomena problem.

Dorothy Kilgallen was the most famous syndicated woman journalist of her day. Stationed in England in 1954 - 55, and privy to the highest levels of English society and its secrets, she wired two unusual dispatches that may have contributed to her death. The first, sent in February 1954, mentioned a "special hush-hush meeting of the world's military heads" scheduled to take place the following summer. The 1955 dispatch, which barely preceded her death from an alleged overdose of sleeping pills and alcohol (a la Marilyn Monroe), quoted an unnamed British official of cabinet rank:

"We believe, on the basis of our inquiry thus far, that saucers were staffed by small men-probably under four feet tall. It's frightening, but there is no denying the flying saucers come from another planet."

Whatever the source (rumored to be the Earl of Mountbatten), this kind of leak in the atmosphere of the mid-50s was an unacceptable leak. It is well to recall that the secret CIA-orchestrated Robertson Panel had met in 1953 and issued the Robertson Report.

Briefly summarized, this document, and the attitudes reflected there, represented a new hard-line attitude to covering up all significant UFO phenomena. The year 1953 and the meeting of the Robertson Panel truly initiated the UFO cover up, as we know it today, with a few extra dollops having been added.

Did Dorothy Kilgallen actually commit accidental suicide? And what about her upcoming interview with Jack Ruby of the JFK assassination? Either one of these scenarios would present a grave danger. There appears to be an excellent chance she had help.

Dr. James McDonald, senior physicist, Institute of Atmospheric Physics and also professor in the Department of Meteorology at the University of Arizona, died in 1971 purportedly of a gunshot wound to the head. There is no one who had worked harder in the 60s than McDonald to convince Congress to hold serious, substantial subcommittee meetings to explore the UFO reality of which he was thoroughly convinced. He was definitely a thorn in the side of those who maintained the official cover-up and, needless to ay, his passing to them would be a blessing.

McDonald, allegedly depressed, shot himself in the head. But, alas, he didn't die. He was wheelchair-ridden but somehow, several months after his first attempt, he allegedly got in an automobile, drove to a pawnshop, purchased another pistol from his wheelchair, drove to the desert and allegedly did himself in. McDonald, there can be no doubt, had made many enemies. The question is: How much did these enemies aid and abet the demise of this most worthy and influential campaigner?

Dr. Morris K. Jessup, April 20, 1959. A scientist who firmly believed in UFOs and who devoted his life to proving their existence; Dr. Jessup was a distinguished astrophysicist. He supervised the installing of the first important telescope in the Southern hemisphere.

Dr. Jessup's theory about UFO's is that they are vehicles by which a pygmy race from outer space visited the Earth millions of years ago. The pygmies built a civilization later destroyed by natural calamity.

Vestiges do exist in the pygmy tribes living on Earth today. Much to his chagrin, the scientific establishment rejected his hypotheses. When Dr. Jessup allegedly committed suicide in Dade County Park, Florida, in 1959, certain alarm bells should have gone off. There is no doubt the well-known author of such influential works as *The Case for the UFO* and *The Expanding Case for the UFO* had been depressed. Things had not been going well for him, and he had, it must be admitted, indicated his gloom to close friends, Ivan Sanderson, the biologist, and Long John Nebel, the well-known New York City radio host. Sanderson reported him disturbed by "a series of strange events" which put him "into a completely insane world of unreality."

Was the reality Jessup was faced with at the time "completely insane" or were there, perhaps, forces driving Jessup to the edge, forces with a plan? Anna Genzlinger thoroughly investigated his death. Her conclusion: "He was under some sort of control." Remember, these were the days of secret governmental mind-control experiments that have only recently been uncovered.

Certain facts about the case raise red flags. For example, no autopsy was performed, contrary to the state law. Sergeant Obenclain, who was on the scene shortly after Jessup's body was discovered, has said for the record, "Everything seemed too professional." The hose from the car exhaust was wired on; and it was, strangely, a washing machine hose. Jessup died at rush hour, with more than the usual amount of traffic passing by. He had been visited by Carlos Allende three days before his death and according to his wife, had been receiving strange and threatening phone calls.

We know the navy was very much interested in what he was doing; and we all know, or should know, it is the ONI (Office of Naval Investigations) that has been in the forefront, from the very beginning, of the UFO cover-up.

And what of particular interest was Jessup investigating at the time? Something that was top secret and would remain so for some time: the Philadelphia Experiment.

Dr. James McDonald tried to convince Congress to look into the UFO situation. He died after shooting himself a short while later. The late astronomer Dr. M. K. Jessup was the first to reveal details of the Philadelphia Experiment; he died a few months later.

Before the 1967 Congress of Scientific Ufologists, Gray Barker, the chairman, received two letters and one phone call telling him that Frank Edwards, the noted radio newscaster and champion of flying saucers, would die during the convention. One day after the meeting was convened there was an announcement that Frank Edwards had succumbed to an "apparent" heart attack. How could anybody know that Edwards was going to die, unless it was planned?

The day was June 24, 1967, and the weather in New York City was brutally hot. But inside the Commodore Hotel an icy shiver swept the audience as Jim Moseley, Chairman of the first World UFO Convention, officially called the Congress of Scientific UFOlogists, made this startling announcement.

"Your attention please," he said. A silence fell over the assembly. "We just heard some shocking news. Frank Edwards, the noted broadcaster and champion of flying saucers, died of a heart attack today. He was 59 years old. I need not remind you of the extremely odd coincidence of this news," Moseley continued, "that Frank Edwards' death occurred 20 years after, to the day, the UFOs first made big headlines in America. It was on June 24, 1947, that Kenneth Arnold made his famous sighting of nine flying saucers."

A single gasp rose from 2,000 throats. Frank Edwards had been a leading champion of the existence of UFOs and had forced the public and the government to pay attention to this puzzling phenomenon. He brought respect to the subject because of his stature as a news reporter. Actually, Frank Edwards died on June 23rd, a few hours before midnight. But the coincidence is still there, as if his death had been timed for that significant date.

Was it chance that two other prominent UFOlogists died on June 24, 1967, while two more died on June 24th of other years. The four were: Arthur Bryant, June 24, 1967: The contactee who claimed to have met three Venusians, including the apparent reincarnation of George Adamski, the most famous contactee in UFOdom.

Richard Church, June 24, 1967: The brilliant young chairman-elect of the UFOlogy group CIGIUFO, and an expert on UFOs.

Frank Scully, June 24, 1964: Scully wrote the first significant book about UFOs, ***Behind the Flying Saucers***, in which he mentioned the "little men" or alien humanoids, electromagnetic power plants of saucer, EM effects, and the Air Force's campaign to hide the truth about UFOs from the public, all "ridiculous" ideas that were later accepted.

Willie Ley, June 24, 1969: A well-known writer on rockets and astronautics, Ley wasn't directly involved in UFOlogy but he wrote about space travel and of course it has been long rumored that flying saucers are space ships.

So we have those directly connected with UFOlogy, plus Ley, all who died on June 24th, three within hours of each other.

It definitely looks like someone was sending a message. As an unhappy sequel to this account, Rep. Rouse, who had been supporting Frank Edwards in his campaign for Congressional attention to the UFO issue, died of a similar heart attack shortly afterwards.

The annals of UFOlogy are frighteningly filled with the deaths of UFOlogists from unusual cancers, heart attacks, questionable suicides and all manner of strange happenings.

George Adamski, April 23, 1965: Victim of a heart attack (according to the death certificate) in Silver Springs, Md. Dead within hours despite emergency treatment. Cremated and buried in Arlington National Cemetery.

Adamski claimed to have seen a flying saucer land in southern California. He said he had spoken to its pilot, a Venusian, in front of witnesses, including George Hunt Williamson. (Williamson disappeared mysteriously in 1965) Adamski also claimed to have traveled to Venus and to have been in telepathic communication with saucermen. He toured the world until his death, lecturing and relaying messages from "our space brothers" to live in brotherhood and peace.

Barney Hill, February 25, 1969: One of the most celebrated contactees along with his wife Betty. John Fuller wrote a book about them, ***The Interrupted Journey***. The title refers to an experience the Hills had in 1961 when they encountered a landed saucer. They remembered nothing of the incident. But later, under hypnosis, they described being conducted aboard the saucer by little humanoids, and undergoing physical examinations. The Hills told their story on TV and in lectures. Their sincerity left little doubt as to the truth of their experience.

Mark Probert, February 22, 1969: The most prominent psychic in BSRA (Borderland Science Research Associates), an organization founded by Meade Layne. Probert acted as a "cosmic telephone" link between Earth and an "inner circle" of departed spirits; these spirits enabled Probert to contact saucermen. Reports of the contacts were then published in the BSRA journal. He never claimed to have seen saucermen in person or to have traveled in saucers.

Dr. George Hunt Williamson: Williamson disappeared while on an anthropological expedition to Peru in 1965. He was noted for his explorations of ancient Indian sites in the Andes, which he suspected were saucer bases, landing fields, and cave headquarters. He believed the saucermen had established the bases and were still there.

Later, he experimented with shortwave radio contact, claiming in 1952, that he had established communications with UFOs. Saucers were observed hovering over his radio shack during these broadcasts. Williamson wrote several books about UFOs, the most noteworthy was *The Road in the Sky*.

Dr. Raymond Bernard, Sept. 10, 1966? The question mark is used because some believe Dr. Bernard is still alive. He produced many books about the inner Earth (*The Hollow Earth*, *The Inner World*, etc.). Bernard believed the inside of the hollow Earth to be inhabited by saucermen, making them "inner Earthians" not extraterrestrials. Their flying saucers fly out of the Earth at the North and South Poles, which, according to Dr. Bernard, are openings into the inner world.

Wilbert B. Smith, December 27, 1962: A leading scientist, he was appointed head of the Canadian government's Project Magnet in 1950; the project was designed to investigate flying saucers, taken seriously by the Canadians at that time. But the press ridiculed the idea, and unsympathetic officials shelved it four years later. Smith claimed to have received telepathic messages from UFOs. He aided UFO groups in their researches; he analyzed the famous "Ottawa chunk" and found traces of "oddities" indicating that it was perhaps dumped from a UFO.

Dr. Olavo T. Fontes, May 9, 1968: Dr. Fontes, a distinguished young Brazilian scientist was South America's foremost UFO booster. He investigated and reported innumerable cases, including the classic Itupai Fortress attack by a UFO using heat rays. Unlike hesitant U.S. scientists, Dr. Fontes boldly challenged the "official" viewpoint. He concluded that saucers were "sizing Earth up" for conquest. He maintained this grim view until his death.

The Rev. Della Larson, October 1965: A contactee who claimed Venusians were living on earth among us. She committed suicide in a rest home by hanging herself with a nylon stocking.

Gloria Lee (Byrd), December 1, 1962: She said space people had told her to go on the fast during which she died.

H. T. Wilkins, 1966: Died following a heart attack and was well-known for his two books on UFOs, *Flying Saucers on the Attack* and *Flying Saucers Uncensored*. Like Dr. Fontes, Wilkins was convinced the saucermen were here not for the benefit of mankind, but instead for the possible conquest of planet Earth.

Dr. Charles A. Maney, November 8, 1965: A scientist who risked his reputation by taking UFOs seriously, he wrote - *Challenge of Unidentified Flying Objects* (in collaboration with Richard Hall of NICAP). A professor at Defiance College in Ohio, he used scientific statistical methods to promote the case for UFOs, and "scolded" science for its indifference toward the UFO phenomena.

Capt. Robert Loftin, November 21, 1968: Ironically, Loftin's book, *Identified Flying Objects*, was published just a few months before his death. In it he demonstrated that aerial flying objects were "identified" – that is, were identified as real, not illusory.

Edgar Jarrold, 1960: Australian UFOlogist who vanished mysteriously.

Marie Ford, suicide: A young UFO enthusiast who found the body of the Rev. Della Larson.

Doug Hanock, 1968, suicide: A UFO researcher who was confined to a mental hospital. He managed to obtain a gun and shot himself.

Damon Runyon, Jr., April 14, 1968, suicide: Son of the famous sports writer. Involved with the investigation of President Kennedy's assassination; and a writer on UFOs. Saucer Scoop said that young Runyon "fell, jumped, or was pushed off" a Washington, D.C., bridge.

Henry F. Koch, 1966: Publicity director of the Universal Research Society of America. He was written up in *Flying Saucers* as having made a UFO sighting on April 3, 1966, and dying mysteriously a few weeks later. The death certificate said of a heart attack. The magazine suggested the cause of death was saucer radiation.

Dr. B. Noel Opan, August 23, 1959: Dr. Opan made a UFO sighting and later was allegedly kidnapped by three Men-in-Black from his home in Wellington, Ontario, Canada. He was never seen again.

Dag Hammarskjold, September 19, 1961: Known for his general "saintliness" as head of the U.N., and no disbeliever in UFOs, Hammarskjold was killed in a plane crash in Southern Rhodesia. A witness, Timothy Kankasa, swore he saw a craft above the airliner. The UFO emitted beams of light resembling a "flashing torch." The question is: Did a UFO tamper electronically with the airliner, causing it to crash?

And this leads us to the broader question: Did UFOs engineer the deaths of those in our above list? Let's examine this carefully before condemning it as utter "nonsense" or an attempt at "sensationalism."

First, various UFOlogists have revealed threats against themselves either from MIBs or other mysterious sources. In the publication *MIB: A Report on the Mysterious Men in Black Who Have Terrorized UFO Witnesses and Investigators in All Parts of the Nation*, Robert S. Easley writes: "The first real act of violence on the part of the 'Three Men' came on February 25, 1968. On that date I had given a UFO lecture to a group of Boy Scouts and their parents. As I was walking out to my car afterwards, at about 9:45 p.m., two men in a car shot me at without any lights on. Later that same evening I received another mysterious phone call . . . 'if you and your buddies are not out of the saucer field by next Sunday we will have to take other means of action (to put you out).'"

Gray Barker, well-known publisher in the UFO field, tells (in **Spacecraft News** #3) how, when investigating the notorious "mothman" rumors near Pt. Pleasant, W. Va., he found a note on his door saying, somewhat ungrammatically, "ABANDON YOUR RESEARCH OR YOU WILL BE REGRET. YOU HAVE BEEN WARNED."

Similar stories have come from dozens of other UFO investigators. They can hardly all be hoaxes or pranks. Somebody, or something, has been threatening those involved with UFOs, threats that in some cases seem to have been fulfilled.

We might also heed the words of John Keel, who more than any other investigator has sought to uncover the mystery of UFOs and MIB's. Keel said in **Saucer Scoop**, that he believes the MIB's to be "the intelligence arm of a large and possibly hostile group;" and that they are professional terrorists. "Among their many duties is the harassment of the UFO researchers who become involved in cases which might reveal too much of the truth."

"Many duties" may well include outright murder of victims, though in such a skillful way that the police aren't aware the murders even occurred. How is this done?

Frank Edwards and Frank Scully presumably died of heart attacks, Wilbert B. Smith and Dr. Olavo Fontes of cancer, and Barney Hill of a brain hemorrhage. All of them died relatively young, none over the age of 59. We will now ask: can heart attacks, cancer and other diseases he induced in people in some unusual way?

Consider this angle on Frank Edwards, as reported by Brad Steiger and Joan Whritenour in **SAGA**: "Edwards was warned to lay off UFO investigation," we (the two authors) were told. "He had been visited by the same three Men in Black that shut up Albert K. Bender" (a former UFO investigator who was hounded into silence by MIBs.

"Nonsense," another delegate said (the authors reported). "Frank had been ill for six months."

"Not true," argued yet another UFOlogist in the **SAGA** article. "Frank has never been ill. Check the obituary. It reads that death was 'apparently' due to a heart attack. How many other researchers have died of an 'apparent' something or other?"

This conversation occurred at the 1967 Congress of Scientific UFOlogists following the announcement of the death of Frank Edwards. And radio personality Long John Nebel, in his book, **The Psychic World Around Us**, tells how Gray Barker, just before the convention, showed him two mysterious unsigned letters stating that Frank Edwards would die during that convention. "On Thursday afternoon," continues Nebel, "just a few hours before he was due at WNBC (for an interview), Barker phoned again. 'John,' he said, 'something happened a few minutes ago that really shook me up! I got a phone call from a man who said that Edwards would not live to see the end of the convention.

That's all he said before he hung up. The tone of his voice scared me. It was like nothing I've ever heard before, like something not human!"

So before the convention and before June 23 when Edwards died, Gray Barker is on record as having received two letters and one phone call, all predicting the death of the newsman. How could anybody know Edwards would die in advance unless it was planned? How was the heart attack induced?

We must also ask ourselves if all the heart attack cases, plus those involving cancer, brain hemorrhages, and pneumonia should be suspect? And even if such "natural" deaths can be induced, suicide would still be easier to accomplish. You can't tell a man (hypnotically or by telepathy) to have a heart attack, but you can tell him to take his own life.

This brings us to the greatest mystery of all, the alleged suicide of Dr. Morris K. Jessup. Most of his closest friends had no idea he would kill himself. But John P. Bessor, one of Jessup's intimates, points out that Jessup was a very "disappointed" and "discouraged" man, over his losing battle to make UFOs "respectable" among scientists.

Capt. Bruce Cathie of Australia, author of *Harmonic 33* (about a UFO "grid" around earth), says, "When Dr. Morris K. Jessup died in 1959, he had just completed a long and detailed report claiming to prove that the U.S. Navy, during a top secret wartime experiment, caused a warship and its crew to become invisible . . . That, the full story has not yet been released is due, in part, to a restriction imposed by Dr. Jessup himself, when he decreed that his report should not be published less than five years and not more than 10 years after his death.

The present ending to his story is as fantastic as the invisible ship itself. In 1959, Dr. Jessup handed all his documents on the case to a close friend to be held in trust, and he then headed for a holiday in Florida . . . Three days later he was found dead in his car."

However, Gray Barker, in his book, *The Strange Case of Dr. M. K. Jessup*, gives the most startling data. He reports that Richard Ogden, a UFO researcher of Seattle, Wash., sent a message saying, in part: "Now as for Jessup, his suicide was a frame-up. Jessup fell victim to hypnotism. He was sent a tape-recording that contained self-destruction suggestions . . .This is what happened to Jessup. It was cold-blooded murder!"

Ogden never documented his claims so the validity of his charges is open to question. But Jessup did write "suicide notes" to several of his friends, including Long John Nebel.

The most intriguing of the suicide theories stems from the fact that Jessup was a great friend of the medium, Mark Probert, and believed in spirit communications. Members of BSRA said that before his death, Jessup gave a strange farewell comment: "I go to prove for myself the reality of worlds beyond time and space." After Jessup's death, Probert received a long scientific dissertation on life-after-death but the sender would not name himself, but hinted that it was indeed Jessup. Jessup always seemed to be a special target for weird happenings. A copy of his book, *The Case for the UFO*, was returned with marginal notes throughout, made by three men who referred to themselves as "aliens." Many of their notations indicated they knew superscience and were familiar with saucer craft. This marked copy was sent to the Navy, which took it seriously and consulted Dr. Jessup, who could throw no light on the mystery.

Jessup also received letters from a "Carlos Allende" (the famous "Allende Letters" case) referring to a Navy ship becoming invisible and being teleported from one city to another. This mystery was never cleared up. The whole Jessup affair remains an unsolved riddle to this day.

Another riddle is the strange disappearance of Dr. Raymond Bernard. Dr. Bernard lived his later life on the island of Santa Catarina, off the coast of Brazil. Although he himself never reached the "inner world" he wrote about, he claimed to know others who did, and who disappeared before they could lead him below.

Bernard once wrote UFO researcher, Timothy Beckley, that his (Bernard's) life was in constant danger from the inner-earth beings. Bernard presumably died at his home in December 1966, but Gray Barker said: " . . . efforts to obtain a copy of the death certificate, or proper information from the American Embassy, have been to no avail." Bernard said he would allow Barker to publish his book, *The Hollow Earth*, only if he had died or was "successful in finding an entrance into the inner earth." This was included in Barker's brochure for the book, *Was Dr. Bernard Swallowed up by the Inner Earth?* Thus we don't know if Dr. Raymond Bernard is buried six feet under, or 1,000 miles under.

It should be noted that the infamous MJ-12 papers states that many military and government personnel had been terminated (murdered without due process of law) when they had attempted to reveal the secret of UFOs. If you consider the controversial papers to be actual top-secret documents, this could be at least one source that clearly reveals what has happened to those who dare get to close to the UFO secret.

SOME RECENT NAMES TO THE EVER-GROWING LIST

Unfortunately, the trend of unusual deaths for UFO witnesses and investigators has continued in the subsequent years with no sign of letting up. It came as a complete shock for many upon hearing of the unexpected death of writer Jim Keith. Keith, known for such cult-favorite books as *Black Helicopters Over America*, *Casebook On Alternative 3*, and *The Gemstone Files*, had been hospitalized after accidentally hurting his leg at the Burning Man Festival.

Thinking it was just a bad sprain; Keith went home and tried to sleep it off. The next morning Keith realized that his leg was in worse shape than he had earlier assumed.

Keith called the paramedics who took him to Washoe Medical in Reno, Nevada. The doctors examined Keith and scheduled him for surgery to fix a fractured tibia. Jim was uneasy about being put under with anesthesia and told his nephew, Chris Davis, that he had the feeling that if they put him under he would die. The doctors insisted, however, that the operation was routine and completely safe.

According to Keith's friend, Kenn Thomas, on September 7, 1999, a blood clot traveled from Jim Keith's leg to his lung during or shortly after surgery and killed him. Washoe County deputy coroner Steve Finnell told a reporter from the Reno *Gazette-Journal* that there was "no conspiracy" and that Jim's death was considered accidental.

In his book, *The Octopus: Secret Government and the Death of Danny Casolaro* (co-written by Keith, Feral House, 2004), Thomas relates the odd circumstances around a column that Keith had written for *Nitro News* about Princess Diana being pregnant at the time of her death. Even odder was the fact that shortly after Keith's death, *Nitro News*, along with Keith's posted column, went mysteriously offline for two weeks.

The strange coincidences surrounding the unexpected death of Jim Keith continued with the equally strange death of publisher Ron Bonds, whose company IllumiNet Press, published a majority of Jim Keith's books. On April 7, 2001, Bonds and his wife went to eat at an El Azteca restaurant in Lilburn, Georgia. Later that evening Bonds was stricken with attacks of nausea, diarrhea and vomiting.

Bonds soon lapsed into unconsciousness and was taken by ambulance to Grady Memorial Hospital. Despite the best efforts by the emergency room doctors, Bonds died from massive swelling and bleeding of his stomach and colon. The autopsy revealed that Bonds had died from complications brought about by the bacteria *clostridium perfringens*. Health inspectors discovered that the beef served at the El Azteca restaurant was contaminated with the dangerous bacteria.

Kenn Thomas also notes in *The Octopus* that in November 2001, suspicious circumstances surrounding knee-surgery operations where the patients were infected with the clostridium bacteria were traced to a tissue bank in Atlanta, near Ron Bonds home.

"How odd," writes Thomas, "that Keith's friend and publisher died of poisoning from the same bacteria, that many knee injuries ended in death due to clostridium, and that clostridium caused 'blackleg' in cattle, a term that resonated eerily with the knee injury that claimed Keith's life."

The strange deaths, unfortunately, continued when Sherry Marie Yearsley, the mother of Jim Keith's two daughters, was found dead along a Reno highway in June 2002. Yearsley's partially clothed body was discovered shortly before noon near the railroad tracks that run along the south side of the interstate 80 in Nevada.

According to police Lt. Ken Lightfoot, Yearsley's death is considered suspicious and that the woman did not get to the site on her own: "We think it was a dump," he said. Yearsley had been dead probably less than a day when passengers on a passing Amtrak train spotted the body

To this day, no official explanation has ever been offered on who killed Sherry Yearsley or why. It takes no great stretch of the imagination to wonder if Yearsley was murdered because of her past relationship with Jim Keith.

Strange and Unexplained Deaths at the Hands of the Secret Government

The death of Jim Keith, while unusual, could have been accidental. However, the shooting death of writer and secret government nemesis William Cooper on November 5, 2001, was by no means an accident.

William Cooper was probably best known for his explosive book: ***Behold A Pale Horse***, (1991 Light Technology Publishing), where he was one of the first to publicly announce that there was a government cover-up concerning UFOs. At first, Cooper, along with John Lear and others, was convinced that the United States government had fallen into an unholy alliance with extraterrestrial creatures, with the innocent citizens of planet Earth as their unwitting pawns. He would later change his mind and declare that the whole "extraterrestrials in league with the U.S. government" was a massive disinformation campaign by the New World Order.

The fact that Cooper died a violent death came as no surprise to those who knew him. Writer Bill Hamilton remarked that he had predicted years ago that Cooper's life would end violently because he had a real love for firearms and booze, and had a difficult time distinguishing truth from fantasy.

Anyone who ever dealt with Bill Cooper would always be left with a definite opinion of the man. His strong convictions and abrasive personality irritated even his closest friends, and those who were not experienced with dealing with the man could be left befuddled and angry by the encounter.

In recent years, Cooper had become increasingly belligerent and confrontational with anyone and anything that he perceived represented the sham-government. He refused to pay taxes and threatened people with his ever-present pistol. Finally, federal arrest warrants were issued for him and his wife. In 1998, Cooper published what essentially was a manifesto on the unconstitutionality of the IRS. In this, Cooper publicly warned that any attempts by the government to execute the arrest warrants would be met with armed resistance. The writing was already on the wall.

On November 5, 2001, the quiet night around the Cooper house was suddenly shattered by the sound of loud music, laughter, and the grinding cacophony of pickup truck engines. It wasn't the first time that teenagers, looking for a secluded place to party had parked on the road leading to the house. And like before, Bill grabbed his gun and got into his car, heading down the lane to chase the intruders away.

However, these intruders were not who they seemed, and they were waiting for Cooper. They knew what he was ready to do. What he had always said he would do. And they knew what they had to do. All they needed was for Cooper to make the first move.

According to the ***Round Valley Paper***, around midnight, local police with a warrant for a couple of aggravated-assault warrants went up in force to Bill Cooper's house, letting on to be teenagers drinking and partying, with the radio turned up loud.

Bill came out of his house and drove over to them, demanding that they get off of his mountain. Two officers jumped Bill in his car. Bill backed it up, shoved one officer out and shot the other one twice in the head with his 45-hand gun.

Cooper then exited his vehicle and began running toward the house, firing shots with a handgun toward the deputies. Nowhere in the police report did it mention that Cooper only had one leg – the other lost in combat long ago. At that point, another sheriff's deputy who had been at the side of Cooper's home, approached Cooper and opened fire, killing him instantly.

Cooper had made it known that he would take action against law enforcement from years back stating, "Trespassers will be shot on discovery." He also denied violating any laws during that period as well.

Cooper had a history of harassing and threatening local residents with deadly force. He had been charged with aggravated assault and endangerment, as well as being wanted by the U.S. Marshall's Service on unrelated felony charges. Cooper had spent his last month challenging the government's claims about what caused the destruction of the World Trade Center on September 11.

Most who knew Cooper all state that he was a hard man to get along with – if at all. His demeanor and attitude was "unfriendly" at best. Although state-sponsored media called Cooper a: "national militia leader," no one has yet to come forward who was under his command, nor has anyone to this point come forward to claim his 'militia rank.'

The Patriot Act of 2001 had many wondering if the Cooper take down was just the beginning in silencing the voices on opposition in the Country. "Are they just starting in alphabetical order?" one person asked. Cooper certainly could have riled the secret government because he was the first to provide evidence of explosives being found inside the Murrah Building in Oklahoma City on April 19, 1995, including the type of explosive used.

Was the death of William Milton Cooper the result of a conspiracy to silence those who strive to make a complacent world aware of the evil that lies just underneath the veneer of our society – or simply the death of a man whose acquaintances had always known would end his life in violence and bloodshed?

It should also be noted that also in 2001, writer and researcher Branton, known for his book **The Dulce Wars** (1999, Global Communications), was critically injured in a mysterious hit-and-run accident. Suffering severe head-injuries, Branton remained in a coma for several weeks, but finally regained consciousness thanks to the efforts of his parents and fans worldwide.

Could it be that some group with a secret to keep targeted all the people listed in this chapter for death? A secret that is so terrible that someone is willing to kill for it? It seems that the answer to this question is a shocking YES. Witnesses, researchers, and writers of the UFO phenomena are being harassed and singled out for elimination because of something that they either knew, or were on the verge of discovering.

What makes this especially surprising is the fact that military and government spokespeople have been saying for years that there are no such things as UFOs. If this was true, it seems that someone is very interested in keeping investigators away from something that is nothing more than a figment of the imagination. Their words may say one thing, but it is their actions that say another. These actions say that seeing and investigating UFOs is a dangerous thing and should be done with extreme caution.

CHAPTER FOUR
The Plane Truth

Statisticians are often fond of pointing out that with all of the modes of transportation, plane travel is definitely the safest. Everyday, thousands of commercial and private flights take place with few of the problems that occur with ground vehicles like automobiles and commercial trucks. Because of these statistics it is odd that an inordinate number of politicians (and musicians) have met their fate due to an airplane accident.

For arguments sake it should be pointed out that many politicians and musicians travel extensively by plane, especially small private and commuter planes that do have more accidents than the larger commercial jets. However, the accidental death of any politician should be scrutinized extremely carefully, considering that in the United States, politicians that stand out and make waves in the status quo tend to die off rather quickly.

What makes the plane crash scenario so perfect in eliminating political enemies is that the mainstream media tends to accept an airplane crash as merely and accident and failing to conduct any investigations on their own. It is a conspiracy of unasked questions and abandoned investigative leads.

Many recent plane crashes have been deemed accidents by the authorities and reported as such by the media before any investigation was started. More than the circumstances and evidence surrounding any particular crash, it is this pattern of pre-emptive reporting which should arouse the public's suspicions.

For the purposes of a cover-up, management of public opinion is even more important than control of the evidence, especially when the most important evidence is circumstantial and immediately obvious to anybody who cares to think about it: the timing of the crash and the identity of the victim(s). In cases when a death in a crash has a direct effect on the balance of political power in the government, here is a question which must always be asked, and almost never is: "Is it possible that this particular airplane crash was actually an act of sabotage, a political assassination?

CONGRESSMAN HALE BOGGS:
DARED TO QUESTION THE WARREN COMMISSION

Congressman Hale Boggs, who served 27 years as a Louisiana representative, sat on the Warren Commission, which concluded that President JFK was slain by a lone assassin and that there was no conspiracy. As more facts came out in the late 1960s, Boggs is said to have become distressed over ever being involved with the Commission, per his wife in testimony before the Assassination Records Review Board in 1997.

Boggs was genuine in his convictions, possibly the last of the ethical grass roots politicians who survived in Washington not because he was a shark, but because he was so affable that probably no one felt threatened by him. He led the movement in Congress to have a House Investigation of the assassination, but backed down after LBJ persuaded Boggs that too many independent investigations would not be a good thing. LBJ's appointment of Boggs to the Commission was therefore the "politically correct" thing to do, in addition to the fact that Boggs was a ranking Democrat in Congress.

Later, in 1971 and '72, Boggs began complaining that the Warren Report was a whitewash and that J. Edgar Hoover's FBI not only helped cover up the JFK murder but blackmailed Congress with massive wire-tapping and spying.

Boggs believed that Warren Commission staff member Arlen Specter was a major cover-up artist for the Warren Report, and that Specter created the fake scenario of "the magic bullet," to frame the dead Lee Harvey Oswald as the lone assassin. As Democratic House Majority Leader, Hale Boggs was positioned to become Speaker of the House and, therefore, in the line of succession to the Presidency. In a speech in 1971, Boggs accused the FBI of tapping his phone and publicly denounced the Bureaus "Gestapo tactics" saying that as a result, America was no longer "free." On the other side of the aisle, defending Hoover, Congressman Ford, challenging Boggs to prove his claims.

Boggs knew that Richard M. Nixon was in or near Dallas from several days before the JFK murder to late that day, Nixon being part of the military and CIA planning group. To supervise the assassination, the group met on the nearby ranch of Nixon's crony, Clint Murchison the oilman, as described in the book **Farewell America**, written under the pen name James Hepburn, and published about 1969. **Farewell America** was a bestseller in Europe but suppressed in the U.S. In the appendix of the book is the only known list of secret JFK political assassination documents, implicating the CIA, in the National Archives.

Sherman Skolnick was on a Dallas radio show with a former Director of Pepsico Bottlers, whose counsel in 1963 was Nixon. He said Nixon did not leave that morning and when the murder was announced, Nixon, unlike the others gathered for a business convention, wanted to continue conducting business as usual as if nothing had happened.

On Oct. 16, 1972, a month before Nixon was re-elected President, Congressman Boggs' plane disappeared on a flight to Alaska. Privately, investigators later said the plane was found, but the monopoly press, the military, and the CIA publicly proclaimed the plane could not be located.

However, fresh controversy surrounds the plane crash as new information obtained through an FBI report revealed that a tip concerning the location of the downed plane might never have been pursued. The FBI telex was sent to the Washington, D.C. FBI headquarters where it was presumably passed to the Acting Director, L. Patrick Gray. The previous director, J. Edgar Hoover, had been in a significant conflict with Boggs, who called for his resignation on the floor of the Congress. Boggs was one of the most powerful people in the country at a time when misuse of power was just beginning to be seen, culminating in the resignation of the President of the United States Richard Nixon.

Despite the new development, however, Alaska State Troopers said they would not mount a renewed effort to find the wreckage of the Cessna-310 that carried Boggs, the former House Majority Leader, and an Alaska congressman, Nick Begich.

Col. John Murphy, director of the troopers, said it would be nearly impossible to find the plane.

"We have taken the time necessary to research the new information received and to review old files, but have determined that to search the coordinate indicated from the radio tracking almost 20 years prior would have negligible results," Murphy said in a statement.

Begich, Boggs, and two others were flying from Anchorage to Juneau when their plane disappeared in a storm near the Malaspina Glacier. The plane was never found despite an intensive search.

A Washington, D.C. newspaper, **Roll Call**, through a Freedom Of Information Act request, found the existence of the FBI report and questioned whether anyone followed up on the lead immediately following the plane's disappearance.

"The FBI documents on the report leave unresolved the question of whether (the tip) was followed up in the days after the crash, and those most familiar with the massive search have no recollection of hearing about it," the newspaper reported.

The Coast Guard reviewed its records of the original search after the newspaper report and found no evidence of the tip, a spokesman said. The agency decided not to look for the plane again, although pilots that fly near the area on other missions have been instructed to look for the wreckage.

Mark Begich, the late congressman's son and an Anchorage city councilman, said he would like the questions surrounding his father's disappearance to be answered.

"We just want to know if they followed this up at the time," Begich said. "If not, why not? If so, what did they find?"

Mark Begich also praised the troopers for reviewing the case.

"For the troopers to take a look into it was worthy, whereas the Coast Guard said 'We're not interested,'" he said.

Mark Begich said his brother had written a letter to Alaska Sen. Ted Stevens asking him to push authorities for more information on the tip. The source of the lead was blacked out on the FBI documents **Roll Call** obtained, according to the newspaper.

Begich said the tip came from someone in Long Beach, Calif., an area where a lot of military equipment was tested, including heat-detection devices that could have generated the lead that **Roll Call** unearthed.

Rumors have circulated for years that Rep. Boggs, along with Rep. Nicholas J. Begich, survived the sabotage that caused their plane to crash. They were allegedly picked up by a CIA "rescue team" and either murdered on the spot or were taken to an undisclosed location outside of the U.S. where they remained imprisoned until they finally died of natural causes.

One interesting point surrounding the disappearance include the fact that Boggs was taken to the airport for the first leg of the trip by a young democrat named Bill Clinton who later, as President, appointed Congressman Boggs' wife, Lindy, to the position of U.S. Ambassador to the Vatican after she served eighteen years in the Congress after her husband's disappearance.

```
AUG-03-1992  12:18  FROM  ROLL CALL NEWSPAPER      TO       190727-6591?5    P.02
```

```
     R089 LA PLAIN
     128PM URGENT 10-18-72 ALD
  TO ACTING DIRECTOR
     ATTN: GENERAL INVESTIGATIVE DIVISION
     ANCHORAGE VIA WASHINGTON
  FROM LOS ANGELES (62-NEW) 2P

  CONGRESSMAN HALE BOGGS DASH DEMOCRAT, LOUISIANA;
  CONGRESSMAN AT LARGE NICK BEGICH DASH DEMOCRAT, ALASKA;
  RUSSEL BROWN; MISCELLANEOUS INFORMATION CONCERNING.

        REMYTEL TODAY,

                TELEPHONICALLY ADVISED AT EIGHT FIFTYONE
  AM, TODAY, THAT HE HAD BEEN CONTACTED BY
  WHO INFORMED       THAT AFTER THE FIRST REPORT WAS RECEIVED
  THE INFORMATION CONCERNING THE LOCATION OF THE DOWNED AIR-
  CRAFT WAS CHECKED WITH A LARGER UNIT.  THE LARGER UNIT NOW
  DISCLOSES THE DOWNED AIRCRAFT IS AT THE FOLLOWING LOCATION:
     QUOTE DRAW A STRAIGHT LINE FROM ANCHORAGE TO JUNEAU;
  HEAD WEST FROM JUNEAU TWO HUNDRED AND FIFTYSIX AND ONE-HALF
  MILES CROSS YAKUTAT BAY AND THE MALASPINA GLACIER; TWELVE
  POINT EIGHTYSEVEN MILES FROM THE GLACIER, DRAW A LINE FROM THAT

  ENDPAGE ONE
```

A recently uncovered FBI telex indicates that despite a tip on the whereabouts of Boggs plane, nothing was done to follow it up.

AUG-20-1992 18:11 FROM ROLL CALL NEWSPAPER TO 19072746.25175 P.02

PAGE TWO
LA-62-NEW
-POINT TO THE COAST, GO BACK NORTH ALONG THAT LINE SIX POINT
FORTY THREE MILES TO THE DOWNED AIRPLANE. UNQUOTE

    THIS INFORMATION WAS IMMEDIATELY FURNISHED TO ▇▇▇▇▇▇ b2c

▇▇▇▇▇▇▇▇▇▇▇▇, U. S. COAST GUARD, LOS ANGELES.
AT NINE TEN AM ▇▇▇▇ TELEPHONICALLY RECONTACTED LOS ANGELES
FBI OFFICE AND FURNISHED FOLLOWING INFORMATION: b2c b2D

    QUOTE TRACKING EQUIPMENT NOW BEING USED IS TRACKING THE
MEN AND NOT THE PLANE. UNQUOTE

    ▇▇▇▇ STATED THIS INFORMATION MAY BE SIGNIFICANT, AND SUGGESTS
PASSENGERS HAD DEPARTED DOWNED PLANE. AT THIS TIME
INQUIRY MADE OF ▇▇▇▇ IF HE WOULD SUBMIT TO PERSONAL INTERVIEW b2c b2D
-FOR FULL DETAILS AND HE REPLIED QUOTE NO UNQUOTE.

    ABOVE INFORMATION IMMEDIATELY FURNISHED ▇▇▇▇▇▇▇▇▇▇
U. S. COAST GUARD.

END

R RELAY
DKS FBI WASHDC CLR

THE DANGERS MONTANA POLITICS

Many elected officials say they've had a few close calls traveling by airplane or car to perform their jobs or campaign, but they try not to dwell on them. Most say that flying in small planes often is a necessary part of politics, despite the tragic crashes that have killed many of their colleagues.

"If I worried about the dangers we're in or the close calls, I'd never go anywhere," said Montana Lt. Gov. Judy Martz. "I operate on the positive part. I just don't think about the negative."

Officials in Montana have a lot to consider when it comes to politics and plane travel. On January 25 1962, Montana Governor Don Nutter boarded a National Guard Airplane to fly to Cutbank to speak at a Chamber of Commerce banquet. The planes wing broke off flying through Wolf Creek canyon. High winds and the age of the plane were contributing factors in the crash. Others who perished along with the Governor were Edward Wren – Secretary of Agriculture, Dennis Gordon – Nutter's executive Secretary and three National Guard Airmen.

Montana Secretary of State James (Jim) Waltermire, while running for governor, was killed on April 8, 1988 in a plane crash near Helena, Montana while returning from a campaign appearance. As well, Cecil Franklin Weeding, a Democratic member of Montana State House of Representatives, 1970-72; and a member of Montana State Senate from 1985-94, who was a candidate for the Public Service Commission in the Democratic primary election, was killed in a plane crash near Lodge Pole, Montana on May 6, 1998.

It has been alleged that Weeding knew about drug operations and corruption that involved some of the leading figures in Montana and the U.S. government and was planning on revealing what he knew in an upcoming press conference. Unfortunately, he died before he could reveal what he knew.

The widow of Governor Don Nutter never changed her steadfast opinion that Governor Nutter had been assassinated. Until the rule of organized crime in Montana and the U.S. is broken, we are forced to live in a time of fear when we are killed on the orders of evil men. It seems obvious that foul play was involved in the death of candidate Weeding. The tragic death comes in unique harmony with many other strange occurrences in Montana and other states across the country.

WAS SECRETARY OF COMMERCE RON BROWN MURDERED?

On April 3 1996, U.S. Secretary of Commerce Ron Brown perished along with 34 others on a trade mission to the Balkans when their U.S. Air Force Boeing 737 crashed into a mountain near Croatia's Dubrovnik airport. When the U.S. military arrived at the scene, Croatian soldiers were already there, and there is evidence that the site had been looted. The Air Force, in a 22-volume report issued in June of 1996, confirmed its initial judgment that the crash resulted from pilot errors and faulty navigation equipment.

Questions began to be asked when discrepancies in the Air Forces report were uncovered. Despite good evidence that something other than an accident took the lives of Brown and 34 others, the Air Force and government have not wavered with their original determination.

The late Ron Brown, was the first African American to hold the office of U.S. Secretary of Commerce, Secretary Brown was born in Washington, D.C. in 1941. He grew up in New York, and with the help of a scholarship attended Middlebury College in Vermont. He received his law degree from St. John's University, attending at night while working by day as a welfare caseworker for the City of New York. He served for four years in the Army in both Germany and Korea.

As a lawyer, a negotiator, a pragmatic bridge builder, and the highly successful immediate past chairman of the Democratic National Committee, Secretary Brown brought wide experience to the newest challenge of building a strong private sector/public sector partnership. "The Department of Commerce's central mission must be to promote long-term economic growth," he had once stated. "That includes rebuilding our industrial base and working with small business owners and minority entrepreneurs to create and expand employment opportunities."

Secretary Brown served on President Bill Clinton's National Economic Council, the Domestic Policy Council and the Task Force on National Health Care Reform. He was also chairman of the Trade Promotion Coordinating Committee, the Co-Chair of the U.S.-Russia Business Development Committee and the U.S.-Israel Science and Technology Commission, and lead President Clinton's initiative on the revitalization of the California economy.

Just before his death, Brown was scheduled to testify in a campaign finance scandal related to one of his employees, James Huang, who had been a multimillion dollar fundraiser for the Democrats before entering public service, and possibly afterward as well. As a government employee, Huang had been given access to high-level information and sat in on classified presidential briefings. He was suspected by some of funneling money from the Chinese government to the Clinton campaign apparatus.

Even though the China claim was never proved, Huang pleaded guilty to felony campaign violations. There was also more than a suggestion that DNC fund-raising had wormed its way into the decision-making at the Commerce Department, courtesy of Secretary Brown. Subpoenas were flying in the probe, with the names of Brown and his son Michael listed among those scheduled to receive such subpoenas,

An independent counsel investigation was launched against Brown, but it was little noticed until early April 1996. In the first week of April, Brown delayed his testimony in a court proceeding related to the Huang case by one week, so that he could fly to Bosnia-Croatia on a trade mission. But Brown's death brought a close to the investigation of any financial improprieties.

Press reports state that at time of the crash "the worst storm in a decade was raging" when, in fact, an Air Force investigation concluded "the weather was not a substantially contributing factor to this mishap?" In the minutes before Brown's plane crashed, five other planes landed without difficulty at the same airport.

Brown's plane was piloted by seasoned pilots with many hours of flying time in such an aircraft. Could it be that the Brown plane was misled by ground navigational aids? If so we may never know for the airport maintenance chief at the Croatian airport died from gunshot wounds just three days later. Officials have said his death was a suicide.

The Air Force's investigative report reveals that a backup portable navigation beacon at the airport had been stolen before the crash and never recovered. Could the Brown plane have been "spoofed" - which is aviation vernacular for using a spurious navigational aid to trick a pilot to change course?

The scientific investigation began on the gurney at Dover Air Force base where Secretary Brown's body lay some four days after his death. As Chief Petty Officer Kathleen Janoski, then a photographer for the Armed Forces Institute of Pathology, and a member of the United States Navy for twenty-two years, says that she looked at Ron Brown's skull and exclaimed: "Look at the hole in Ron Brown's head. It looks like a gunshot wound."

Among those who took a look at the wound was United States Army Lt. Colonel David Hause, a deputy medical examiner with the A.F.I.P. Hause agreed with Janoski that the head wound appeared to be a gunshot wound and added that it "looked like a punched-out .45-caliber entrance hole." But the A.F.I.P.'s Colonel William Gormley, the pathologist who was examining Brown's body did not concur with the Janoski-Hause evaluation.

Lt. Col. Steve Cogswell, a senior pathologist with the Armed Forces Institute of Pathology, told the Pittsburgh Tribune Review that Ron Brown had sustained a suspicious head wound, an inwardly beveling .45 caliber hole that resembled a gunshot wound. Cogswell had photographs of X-rays to support his observations. He revealed that Ron Brown's body was never autopsied despite the unexplained wound.

Former NYPD investigator and forensics professor Tom Cubic told United Press International that if there is any doubt about the cause of death, such as an injury that looks like a bullet wound, an autopsy should always be done. In response to press criticism of his agency's handling of the death of Brown, Dr. Jerry Spencer, the chief medical examiner for the U.S. armed forces, issued a sweeping gag order on military and civilian personnel in his office.

Just before the gag order was issued, Lt. Col. Cogswell Cogswell was escorted to his home by an Air Force police officer that demanded entry to his house while Cogswell retrieved case materials in his possession. One AFIP staff member said that the treatment of Cogswell was "unheard of" for a military officer and likened the restrictions on his movements to "house arrest."

All those who have espoused the possibility of homicide in Brown's demise have been silenced by the military in one way or another. Chief Petty Officer Janoski, the prime whistle blower, has further fueled a conspiracy flame by pointing to the fact that the X-rays of Brown's skull has vanished. Other body X-rays are still in existence but the whereabouts of the skull X-rays as they were displayed in the light box at Dover Air Force base is not known. Military investigators stand by their findings that the plane broke up and that Brown was hit in the head by something in the cabin.

Statement from the Armed Forces Institute of Pathology
Regarding the Ron Brown Case

The Armed Forces Institute or [sic] Pathology (AFIP) stands by its findings that former Commerce Secretary Ron Brown died as a result of injuries suffered in the crash of an Air Force CT-43 aircraft in Croatia on April 3, 1996. "Based on my personal examination and the forensic evidence, I am convinced that he died of injuries sustained during the mishap," said Col. (Dr.) William T. Gormley, assistant armed forces medical examiner.

Recent reports suggest that Brown could have been shot prior to the accident and that an autopsy should have been performed. The reports also say an x-ray of Brown's skull contains metal fragments consistent with a gunshot wound. Gormley confirmed the forensic evidence and his personal examination rule out the possibility of a gunshot wound.

"Due to the initial appearance of Brown's injuries," he said, "we carefully considered the possibility of a gunshot wound. However, scientific data, including x-rays, ruled out that possibility," Gormley said.

The alleged "bullet fragments" were actually caused by a defect in the reusable x-ray film cassette, Gormley explained. Medical examiners took multiple x-rays using multiple cassettes and confirmed this finding.

Gormley confirmed there was no gunshot wound, and therefore concluded there was no need for further examination. Had there been the slightest suspicion regarding the nature of Brown's death -- or the death of any other person on the aircraft -- medical examiners would have pursued permission to perform a full internal examination, Gormley said.

Regarding the comments made by LtCol Steven Cogswell and LTC David Hause of the Office of the Armed forces Medical Examiner (OAFME), all AFIP staff members are supposed to coordinate media activities through the public affairs office. Neither man's comments in the Pittsburgh Tribune-Review are those of the Institute, nor were they coordinated with the Institute, and do not reflect AFIP's findings in the case. They've been directed to follow standard procedure and refer media inquiries to the public affairs office during normal working hours.

Punitive actions have not been taken against Dr. Cogswell and he is not under house arrest. The Institute has convened an internal investigation to make sure that no other internal policies or procedures were violated -- unrelated to the forensic findings -- and it is important that Dr. Cogswell be available during this review. He's therefore been directed to stay at his normal duty station during regular working hours.

"These reports bring unnecessary grief to the families of those who died in this tragic accident," Lt. Gen. (Dr.) Charles H. Roadman II, the Air Force surgeon general said. "The Air Force and the Armed Forces Institute of Pathology offer our sympathies to the families of all those killed for this undue intrusion into their private lives."

Department of Defense Armed Forces Institute of Pathology Washington, DC 20306-6000 Contact: Chris Kelly, AFIP Public Affairs Director – 12/9/1997

TOP: Brown's plane was piloted by seasoned pilots. Could it be that the plane was misled by ground navigational aids?

BOTTOM: With the exception of a few that have circulated on the net, X-Rays of Brown's skull with the odd wound has vanished.

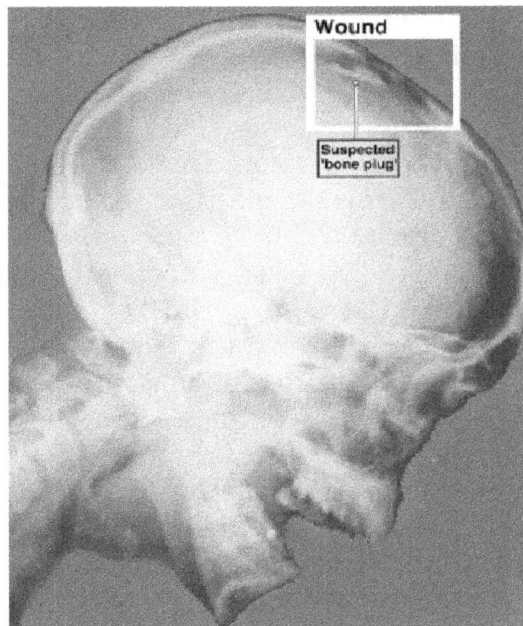

MISSOURI GOVERNOR MEL CARNAHAN

Missouri governor and U.S. Senate candidate Mel Carnahan, his son and a top adviser were killed on October 17, 2000 in the fiery crash of a private plane about 30 miles south of St. Louis. Difficult conditions hampered more than 100 emergency workers who combed the scattered wreckage of the light aircraft that went down in rain and fog in a densely wooded area about 7:30PM. Members of the governor's security staff were also at the scene.

Carnahan, 66, a Democrat who had been governor of Missouri for eight years, was running for the Senate and was locked in a tight race with incumbent Republican Sen. John Ashcroft. The race had been expected to be close, and was regarded as one of the Democratic Party's best chances to pick up a seat in the Republican-dominated Senate.

U.S. President Bill Clinton, in Egypt for a Middle East peace summit, contacted Carnahan's wife, Jean, after hearing the news. Clinton aides said that Vice President Al Gore also telephoned the governor's wife.

The governor and the other two men were aboard a twin-engine Cessna that had been headed for a campaign stop in New Madrid, in southeastern Missouri. Kansas City Flight Service said the governor's plane took off at 7:06 p.m. from St. Louis Downtown-Parks Airport, a small airport across the Mississippi River in Illinois, for New Madrid, where the governor was due to attend a fundraiser.

Both Carnahan and his son were licensed pilots. Randy Carnahan normally flew the campaign plane for political events, The Associated Press reported. Lambert-St. Louis International Airport in St. Louis was tracking the governor's plane, which disappeared from radar at 7:33 p.m.

The Missouri State Highway Patrol said the plane crashed about 25 miles south of St. Louis in a hilly, wooded area near the towns of Goldman and Barnhart. Capt. Ed Kemp of the Jefferson County Sheriff's Department said wreckage from the accident had been found, "but it was in very small pieces because it's a heavily wooded and rocky terrain and it's spread over a large area."

Because Carnahan's death came so close to the election, Missouri state laws stipulated that the late Governors name be kept on the ballot. The Ashcroft team was almost guaranteed to win the election. Ashcroft briefly suspended his campaign after Carnahan's death. When he renewed his campaign, he released ads touting himself as a man of "Missouri values" who should lead the state in this time of crisis. He spent the last week of the campaign on a 25-city campaign blitz dubbed the "Show-Me Experience Express" Tour.

In a strange twist, and much to the chagrin of GOP leaders across the country, the late Governor Carnahan won the election, receiving a majority of the ballots and unseating freshman Senator Ashcroft. Acting Missouri Governor Roger Wilson appointed the late Governor's, Jean Carnahan to the seat.

Ashcroft still managed to come out ahead, despite the election of the assassinated Gov. Carnahan, when newly elected President George W. Bush made him Attorney General. It seems that someone wanted John Ashcroft in a high position with the government and no one was going to stand in his way.

U.S. SENATOR PAUL WELLSTONE

U.S. Sen. Paul Wellstone, D-Minnesota, was the Democrat the Bush administration loved to hate. White House political director Karl Rove personally selected Wellstone's Republican challenger in the November 5, 2002 election, former St. Paul Mayor Norm Coleman, with Vice President Dick Cheney and President George W. Bush visiting Minnesota again and again on Coleman's behalf.

But Minnesotans were not taken to the high-level pressure. It seemed that whenever Bush made a swing through the state on Coleman's behalf, it was Wellstone whose poll numbers went up. Actually, Wellstone's numbers had been rising ever since he voted against the president's request for blank-check authorization to launch a war with Iraq.

After months of too-close-to-call poll numbers, the headline of the **Minneapolis Star-Tribune** announced, "Wellstone edges into lead in U.S. Senate race." The **Star-Tribune's** latest poll found the two-term liberal Democratic senator to be ahead by a 47-41 margin among likely voters.

After the poll results were released, a shadowy Virginia group that campaign finance analysts linked to the Bush family and George W. Bush's 2000 campaign, as well as to the insurance and pharmaceutical industries, former Senate Majority Leader Trent Lott and the Republican Party, made a record-breaking $1 million purchase of television and radio advertising time to attack Wellstone. The deceptively named group **Americans For Job Security** was behind the big buy. Headquartered in Alexandria, Virginia, Americans for Security first came on the scene five years ago, when it got started with a $1 million contribution from the American Insurance Association. The American Forest and Paper Association chipped in another $1 million.

Described by the The Annenberg Public Policy Center as a "a tax-exempt conservative, business-backed pro-Republican organization formed in October 1997 to lobby for: reduced taxes, less government regulation, free trade, and downsizing government," it has been linked with a previous initiative by the U.S. Chamber of Commerce and business lobbies that spent $5 million in the 1996 election cycle.

In May, 2000, a **Washington Post** report raised the prospect that Trent Lott was pressuring high-tech lobbyists for contributions to the organization, which that year launched television advertising campaigns attacking the Democratic challengers to several vulnerable Republican senators. (Among the corporations reported to have contributed to Americans for Job Security following that meeting was Microsoft. More recently, pharmaceutical firms have been reported to be prime funders of the group.)

American for Job Security president Michael Dubke refused to reveal the sources of the funding for the attack ads against Wellstone, nor for similar campaigns by the group against Democratic Senators Jean Carnahan and Tim Johnson, who were in tight races in Missouri and South Dakota, respectively. According to Dubke, his organization has "a very strong policy that we don't discuss our members." And elections laws do not appear to require him to do so.

Despite the money that was being poured into Minnesota, Wellstone's poll numbers continued to rise against the republican candidate, former St. Paul Mayor Norm Coleman, who was perceived by Minnesota voters as "White House packaged candidate." Coleman was so despised that Garrison Keillor, the host of the radio show, *A Prairie Home Companion*, referred to Coleman as "this cheap fraud," and, echoing the sentiments of a lot of in-the-know Minnesotans, said of Coleman's political ascension: "To accept it and grin and shake the son of a bitch's hand is to ignore what cannot be ignored if you want your grandchildren to grow up in a country like the one that nurtured and inspired you."

On October 11 2002, Wellstone, the most progressive Democrat in the Senate, voted against the President's war on Iraq, despite a dire personal warning of "severe ramifications" from Vice President Cheney. As the result of his vote, Wellstone's popularity soared. It was clear to the Bush Administration that Wellstone had to be eliminated one way or another.

It seemed as if Vice President Cheney's warning came true, for on October 25 2002, just ten days before his probable election, Sen. Wellstone, his wife Sheila, daughter Marcia, and three staff members, died when their private plane crashed near Evleth, Minnesota. A pilot who witnessed the incident said the twin-engine craft seemed to unexpectedly veer away from the usual approach to the runway.

The crash, which also killed both pilots, came almost two years to the day after a similar plane crash that killed another Democratic Senate hopeful locked in a tight election contest, Missouri Governor Mel Carnahan. The plane, a twin-engine Beechcraft King Air A100, was apparently in good condition when it hit the ground and exploded into flames.

The Beechcraft model has an excellent safety record, with only two fatal crashes, both in December 1997, in the past ten years. Debris recovered from the crash site includes both the plane's engines, which suffered blade damage, suggesting that the engines were running when the plane crashed.

While weather conditions were less than ideal, with some ice and freezing rain, two smaller Beech Queen Air planes had landed at Eveleth without incident two hours before the crash, when temperatures were colder. Wellstone's plane was reportedly equipped with two separate de-icing mechanisms.

Visibility was limited but well above the minimum required—between two and two and a half miles. Although the approach to the airport was being made using instruments, the airport would have been in clear view of the pilot once he descended below the lowest cloud layer at about 700 feet.

The plane's two pilots were both experienced, with the senior man, Capt. Richard Conry, 55, having airline transport pilot certification, the top industry qualification. Co-pilot Michael Guess, 30, was a certified commercial pilot. Wellstone was by all accounts a cautious flier, and there is no suggestion that the decision to fly that day was a reckless one.

The acting chairwoman of the National Transportation Safety Board, Carol Carmody, said there was a slight irregularity in the Eveleth airport's radio beacon, but it was not possible to say whether this contributed to the accident. The plane's altimeter and "possibly one other gauge" were recovered and sent to the NTSB lab in Washington for analysis, but the plane was not required to have a cockpit voice recorder and was not equipped with one.

According to air traffic control records, the flight had proceeded without incident until its last moments. Wellstone's plane took off at 9:37 a.m. from Minneapolis-St. Paul, received permission to climb to 13,000 feet at 9:48 a.m., and received clearance to descend towards Eveleth at 10:01 a.m., at which time the pilot was told there was icing at the 9,000-11,000 foot level. The plane began its descent at 10:10 a.m., passed through the icing altitude without apparent difficulty, and at 10:18 a.m. was cleared for approach to the airport. A minute later, at 3,500 feet, the plane began to drift away from the runway. It was last sighted at 10:21 a.m., flying at 1,800 feet.

Carmody said that the impact area was 300 feet by 190 feet, with evidence of "extreme post-crash fire." The plane apparently was headed south, away from the Eveleth runway, when it hit the ground. "The angle was steeper than would be expected in a normal stabilized standardized approach," she said. Some press reports cited eyewitness accounts of a near-vertical plunge.

The Duluth News Tribune featured a column by Jim Fetzer, a University of Minnesota-Duluth philosophy professor and author, in November 2003. Fetzer wrote that an FBI "recovery team" headed out to investigate the Wellstone plane crash before the plane went down. "I calculate that this team would have had to have left the Twin Cities at about the same time the Wellstone plane was taking off," Fetzer wrote.

Fetzer also noted that Wellstone's plane was "exceptional, the pilots well-qualified, and the weather posed no significant problems." He wrote that: "We have to consider other, less palatable, alternatives, such as small bombs, gas canisters or electromagnetic pulse, radio frequency or High Energy Radio Frequency weapons designed to overwhelm electrical circuitry with an intense electromagnetic field. An abrupt cessation of communication between the plane and the tower took place at about 10:18 a.m., the same time an odd cell phone phenomenon occurred with a driver in the immediate vicinity. This suggests to me the most likely explanation is that one of our new electromagnetic weapons was employed."

Michael Ruppert, publisher of *From the Wilderness*, wrote that the day after the crash he received a message from a former CIA operative who was familiar with those kinds of assassinations. The message read, "As I said earlier, having played ball [and still playing in some respects] with this current crop of reinvigorated old white men, these clowns are nobody to screw around with. There will be a few more strategic accidents. You can be certain of that."

Ruppert also interviewed two Democratic Congress representatives who said they believed Wellstone was murdered. One said, "I don't think there's anyone on the Hill who doesn't suspect it. It's too convenient, too coincidental, too damned obvious. My guess is that some of the less courageous members of the party are thinking about becoming Republicans right now."

Even National Transportation Safety Board officials found aspects of Wellstone's accident puzzling. An article in the *Duluth News Tribune* a few days after the tragedy said that "for some still unexplained reason – [the plane] turned off course and crashed." It quoted Carol Carmody, the NTSB's acting chair and reportedly a former CIA employee, as saying, "We find the whole turn curious."

John Ongaro, a Minnesota lobbyist, wrote to Fetzer about his experience the day Wellstone died. Ongaro said he was driving to the same funeral that Wellstone and his party had been flying to in Eveleth, Minn. While traveling north on Hwy. 53 near the Eveleth-Virginia Municipal Airport in the same area as Wellstone's plane, he received a call on his cell phone at precisely the same time Wellstone's King Air veered off course.

"This call was in a league of its own," Ongaro said. "When I answered it, what I heard sounded like a cross between a roar and a loud humming noise. The noise seemed to be oscillating, and I could not make out any words being spoken. Instead, just this loud, grotesque, sometimes screeching and humming noise."

What he heard may very well have been electronic interference from an EMP or microwave weapon. One writer to talk show host Jeff Rense suggested a scenario involving "black op specialists" in a van or truck full of radio/instrument landing jamming equipment.

"As Wellstone's plane approaches the airport, the VOR/ILS jamming equipment is activated, and a 'decoy' VOR signal is sent to the plane, thus tricking the plane's instruments [and the pilot] into believing the airport is somewhere several degrees off the true course to the runway," S.H. wrote. "The pilot follows that signal straight into the ground. The non-descript van, full of covert electronic jamming equipment, casually leaves the area, looking just like any other TV repair truck or moving van."

One witness of Wellstone's crash, Megen Williams, who lived near the Eveleth airport, told the *St. Paul Pioneer Press* that she heard "a diving noise and then an explosion" as she prepared for work as a nurse in her home near the crash site. At first, she thought it was blasting at a nearby iron ore mine, and she didn't call authorities.

Another local resident, Rodney Allen, said the plane flew right over his house. "It was so close the windows were shaking," Allen said. He added that the craft was "crabbing to the right," then less than a minute later, he felt an impact and heard what he thought sounded like a loud rifle shot.

Investigators from the National Transportation Safety Board said the plane was last seen on air traffic control radar at 10:21 a.m., flying at an elevation of 1,800 feet. Radar tapes indicate Wellstone's plane had descended to about 400 feet and was traveling at only 85 knots near the end of its flight.

Don Sipola, a former president of the Eveleth Virginia Municipal Airport Commission, said "something" caused Wellstone's plan to veer off course at low altitude. "This was a real steep bank, not a nice, gentle don't-spill-the-coffee descent," Siploa said. "This is more like a space shuttle coming down. This was not a controlled descent into the ground."

Wellstone was the target of an apparent assassination plot before. In 2000, as he visited Colombia to survey conditions there, a bomb was found along his route from the airport. He was also sprayed with the herbicide glyphosate by a helicopter above him while watching the Colombian police demonstrate its fumigation of coca plants. Officials called the incident an accident but no investigation was ever conducted.

Wellstone was a vocal opponent of military aid to the Colombian government. While there, he visited human rights activists who said the government did not protect civilians. Wellstone told reporters he thought his Colombian hosts created the bomb story to dissuade him from traveling to certain areas of the country. "I don't know whether I was targeted, but I certainly know that the human rights activists are targeted," Wellstone said.

Among the weird events since Wellstone's death was that his successor in the U.S. Senate, Republican Norm Coleman, was named chairman of the Senate Permanent Subcommittee on Investigations, a practically unheard of position for a freshman senator with no previous experience. Once Coleman was settled in the Senate, his true stripes began to show, and it became clear that, in addition to abandoning Wellstone's political principles, Coleman also rejected his predecessor's reticence about taking political cheap shots at foes – living or dead.

During an interview with the Capitol Hill newspaper **Roll Call**, Coleman waved an unlit cigar in the air and declared: "To be very blunt and God watch over Paul's soul, I am a 99 percent improvement over Paul Wellstone," Coleman told the reporter. "Just about on every issue."

The reporter offered Coleman a chance to redeem himself by asking about the remaining one percent. But Coleman didn't bite. Instead, he complained about Wellstone's political independence. "Wellstone was never with the president," explained Coleman, referring to the Democrat's refusal to go along with the Bush administration's agenda. "I could be with the president most of the time."

The new senator even found time to dismiss the suggestion from some of Wellstone's grieving supporters that his replacement might want to maintain some of his predecessor's legacy. "They lost their champion and they thought something was taken away," Coleman said of Wellstone backers. "All you can do is say, 'Hey, I mourn the loss, but I am here and I am going to do what I think is the right thing to do and thank God I have a chance to be here.'"

U.S. Rep. Betty McCollum, D-Minn., described Coleman's remarks as inappropriate, disrespectful and "an unnecessary attack on a leader our state continues to mourn." She demanded an apology, as did 100 demonstrators who gathered outside Coleman's St. Paul office. Martha Bellou, one of the demonstrators, summed the mood up when she referred to Coleman "defaming the dead" and allowed as how, "Even for Norm this is a new low."

It should be noted that it seems as if someone has declared "open season" on Democratic politicians. In 2001, two leading Senate Democrats, Majority Leader Tom Daschle and Judiciary Committee Chairman Patrick Leahy, were targeted for assassination with letters laced with anthrax. The federal Justice Department—headed by John Ashcroft, who lost to the deceased Mel Carnahan in the Missouri contest—has failed to apprehend the anthrax mailer.

The apparently rigged elections of 2004 that brought in a record number of Republican's to Congress and the Senate, shows that Democrats in the U.S. have become an endangered species. A coup has taken place, and no one noticed.

OTHER PLANE CRASHES OF SIGNIFICANCE

Gary Caradori

Gary Caradori was a retired state police investigator who had been hired by the Nebraska Senate to investigate what the **Washington Times** called "A homosexual prostitution ring."

On the morning of June 29, 1989, **The Times** reported, "A homosexual prostitution ring is under investigation by federal and District authorities and includes among its clients key officials of the Reagan and Bush administrations, military officers, congressional aides and U.S. and foreign businessmen with close ties to Washington's political elite."

Gary Caradori died mysteriously while investigating Lawrence E. King, Jr., a very influential black Republican and close friend of George H.W. Bush. King was director of the Franklin Community Credit Union in Omaha, Nebraska, and was suspected of embezzling $40 million.

Within weeks, the Nebraska Senate found itself questioning child prostitutes, who accused King of running a child prostitution ring. One of these children said that she saw George H.W. Bush at one of King's parties.

Pronto, a newspaper in Barcelona, Spain, reported that the scandal "appears to directly implicate politicos of the state of Nebraska and Washington DC who are very close to the White House and George Bush himself."

On July 11, 1990, Gary Caradori was killed along with his 6-year old son in the crash of his small plane after a mid-air explosion, the cause of which was never discovered. He had told friends repeatedly in the weeks before his death that he was afraid his plane would be sabotaged.

Dan Rocco

Dan Rocco died on April 1, 2002, in a plane crash in Gainesville, Georgia. He was an executive vice president at ChoicePoint, the firm that gained infamy with their faulty "felons" list supplied to Katherine Harris during the 2000 election in Florida. As a result of this list, thousands of voters (mostly African-Americans) were wrongly identified as felons and purged from the rolls.

Charles M. McKee and Matthew Gannon

Charles M. McKee, ostensibly a military attaché for the DIA in Beirut, Matthew Gannon, CIA Deputy Station Chief in Beirut, and three others were on board Pan Am Flight 103, which exploded over Lockerbie, Scotland. They were part of a counterterrorist team in Beirut investigating the possible rescue of nine American hostages in Lebanon.

The McKee team uncovered evidence that a rogue CIA unit called COREA, based in Wiesbaden, was doing business with a man called Monzer Al-Kassar, a Syrian arms dealer and drug trafficker. Al-Kassar was part of the covert network run by U.S. Lieut. Colonel Oliver North. Outraged that the COREA unit in

Wiesbaden was doing business with a Syrian who had close terrorist connections and might endanger their chances of rescuing the hostages, the McKee team decided to fly back to Virginia unannounced and expose the COREA unit's secret deal with al-Kassar. They never got there.

"For three years, I've had a feeling that if Chuck hadn't been on that plane, it wouldn't have been bombed," said Beulah McKee, 75, Charles McKee's mother, to *Time Magazine*. Four months after her son was killed for his efforts to expose the CIA, Mrs. McKee received a sympathy letter from George H. W. Bush. Mrs. McKee has never been satisfied with the government's version of events.

Jake Horton

Jake Horton was a senior vice-president for Gulf Power, a subsidiary of Southern Company (a regional electricity firm and cohort of Enron in the energy industry), and a major contributor to the Bush agenda. Since the turn of the century, American states have kept tight lids on utility monopolies' profits. In the Eighties, consumer groups demanded, rightly, that power companies, including Southern, eat their losses on foolish nuclear investments.

The cash-short company had resorted to such unfortunate tactics as keeping hidden sets of account books tracking non-existent light poles. Horton was told he would be fired and was at the point of testifying to a grand jury about improper payments he made to politicians on the company's behalf. (The company later pleaded guilty to this felony.) He demanded and received use of the corporate jet to confront Southern's directors. Ten minutes after take-off, the jet blew up.

Oct. 6, 2000 – Former state rep. Charles B. Yates of Edgewater Park, Burlington County, N.J. D-Member of New Jersey state senate, 1978-82. Killed, along with his family, in the crash of a small plane he was piloting, near Edgartown, Martha's Vineyard, Dukes County, Mass.

August 4, 2000 – Former State Sen. Thomas Allgood, Sr. Member of Georgia state senate, 1977-91. Killed in the crash of a single-engine airplane, during takeoff from Daniel Field, Augusta, Richmond County, Ga.

March 28, 2000 – Former State Rep. Grover C. Robinson III of Pensacola, Escambia County, Fla. Member of Florida state house of representatives, 1972-84. Died in a helicopter crash at Lake Manapouri, New Zealand.

April 19, 1993: South Dakota Gov. George Mickelson, killed along with seven other people when their state-owned plane crashes in a rainstorm near Dubuque, Iowa.

April 5, 1991 — Former Sen. John Tower, R-Texas, and NASA astronaut Manley "Sonny" Carter Jr. among those killed in the crash of an Atlantic Southeast Airlines flight near Brunswick, Ga.

Strange and Unexplained Deaths at the Hands of the Secret Government

April 4, 1991 – Senator Henry John Heinz III, R-Pittsburgh, Allegheny County, Pa. His widow later married John Forbes Kerry. U.S. Senator from Pennsylvania, 1977-91, was killed when his plane collided with a helicopter over Merion, Montgomery County, Pa.

Aug. 13, 1989 — Rep. Larkin Smith, R-Miss., killed along with his pilot when their Cessna 177 crashes into the DeSoto National Forest in Mississippi.

Aug. 7, 1989 — Rep. Mickey Leland, a Texas Democrat who chaired the House Select Committee on Hunger, killed when plane crashes during a trip to inspect relief efforts in Ethiopia.

Aug. 17, 1988 – Ambassador Arnold Lewis Raphel, U.S. Ambassador to Pakistan, 1987-88, was killed when a plane in which he was a passenger was blown up in midair by terrorists, near Bahawalpur, Pakistan.

Sept. 1, 1983 — Rep. Larry McDonald, D-Ga., was killed when a Russian fighter jet shot down Korean Air Lines Flight 007. His body was lost in the Pacific Ocean and never recovered.

Aug. 2, 1978 — Richard Obenshain, Republican candidate for Senate from Virginia, was killed when plane crashes near Richmond, Va. John Warner, now top Republican on the Senate Armed Services Committee, was picked to run in his place.

Feb. 17, 1977 — Rep. Ralph Frederick Beermann, Republican of Dakota City, Dakota County, Neb. Republican. Died in an airplane crash at the Municipal Airport in Sioux City, Woodbury County, Iowa.

Aug. 3, 1976 – Rep. Jerry Lon Litton, Democrat, while running for U.S. Senator, died in the crash of a private plane, shortly after takeoff from the Municipal Airport Chillicothe, Livingston County, Mo.

Dec. 8, 1972 — Rep. George W. Collins, D-Ill., was killed when his plane crashes on approach to Midway Airport in Chicago. His wife, Cardiss, succeeded him in office.

Both Missouri Governor Mel Carnahan (**TOP**) and
Minnesota Senator Paul Wellstone (**BOTTOM**) died
in suspicious plane crashes.

CHAPTER FIVE
Death in the Fourth Estate

It has never been easy being a journalist. You are expected to write about the truth, but no one really wants to know the truth due to the fact that they have already made up their mind and nothing, not even the facts, is going to dissuade them to consider otherwise. Journalists are mistrusted, maligned, and often accused of having a liberal or conservative bias. Those who do manage to maintain their integrity, and avoid a partisan branding, are usually called weak-willed wimps who cannot defend their own personal opinions. To be a modern journalist is to live on a double-edged sword.

Journalism has arguably reached the lowest point in its history. Ethics and legal scandals are seemingly endless; the press has lost nearly all credibility and public trust; advertising dollars and governmental secrecy have rendered reporters impotent to report the most pressing issues of the day.

On top of the scandals and mistrust, investigative journalists also have to watch their every step to avoid being targeted by those who are not very happy having their dirty laundry revealed for all the world to see. Who knows how many reporters have died mysteriously because they came a little too close to the truth?

Many people will ask why should they care if a few reporters are murdered for asking the tough questions? Why should it matter? It matters because reporters are the most visible exercisers of free speech in Western societies. The content of the news media is in many ways less important than the state of it.

Looking to the press most readily reveals what is happening to all of us; it mirrors who we are, what we are doing, and where we are going. (This is true even for those hardcore anti-liberal-media-bias folks who fail to see that their own anti-liberal bias comes from the media.) If reporters are no longer permitted to operate independently, is anyone?

Wartime press coverage has always been a dangerous mission for a reporter. However, most would never expect to become targets by their own government or allies. Sadly, the new opinion by the U.S. military in the 21st century is that reporters who fail to repeat the government issued propaganda, or who simply get in the way, could find them on the wrong end of a rifle-barrel.

In Iraq, U.S. forces and their Iraqi surrogates are no longer bothering to conceal attacks on civilian targets and are openly eliminating anyone – doctors, clerics, journalists – who dares to count the bodies.

In April 2004, U.S. forces laid siege to Falluja in retaliation for the gruesome killings of four Blackwater employees. The operation was a failure, with U.S. troops eventually handing the city back to resistance forces.

The reason for the withdrawal was that the siege had sparked uprisings across the country, triggered by reports that hundreds of civilians had been killed. This information came from three main sources: 1) Doctors. *USA Today* reported on April 11 that: "Statistics and names of the dead were gathered from four main clinics around the city and from Falluja general hospital". 2) Arab TV journalists. While doctors reported the numbers of dead, it was *al-Jazeera* and *al-Arabiya* that put a human face on those statistics. With unembedded camera crews in Falluja, both networks beamed footage of mutilated women and children throughout Iraq and the Arab-speaking world. 3) Clerics. The reports of high civilian casualties coming from journalists and doctors were seized upon by prominent clerics in Iraq. Many delivered fiery sermons condemning the attack, turning their congregants against US forces and igniting the uprising that forced US troops to withdraw.

U.S. authorities have denied that hundreds of civilians were killed during the siege, and have lashed out at the sources of these reports. For instance, an unnamed "senior American officer," speaking to the *New York Times* labeled Falluja general hospital "a center of propaganda." But the strongest words were reserved for Arab TV networks. When asked about *al-Jazeera* and *al-Arabiya's* reports that hundreds of civilians had been killed in Falluja, Donald Rumsfeld, the U.S. Secretary of Defense, replied that: "what *al-Jazeera* is doing is vicious, inaccurate and inexcusable."

In November 2004, U.S. troops once again laid siege to Falluja – but this time the attack included a new tactic: eliminating the doctors, journalists and clerics who focused public attention on civilian casualties last time around.

The first major operation by U.S. marines and Iraqi soldiers was to storm Falluja general hospital, arresting doctors and placing the facility under military control. *The New York Times* reported that "the hospital was selected as an early target because the American military believed that it was the source of rumors about heavy casual ties," noting that "this time around, the American military intends to fight its own information war, countering or squelching what has been one of the insurgents' most potent weapons."

The Los Angeles Times quoted a doctor as saying that the soldiers "stole the mobile phones" at the hospital – preventing doctors from communicating with the outside world.

But this was not the worst of the attacks on health workers. Two days earlier, a crucial emergency health clinic was bombed to rubble, as well as a medical supplies dispensary next door. Dr. Sami al-Jumaili, who was working in the clinic, says the bombs took the lives of 15 medics, four nurses and 35 patients. *The Los Angeles Times* reported that the manager of Falluja general hospital "had told a U.S. general the location of the downtown makeshift medical center" before it was hit.

Whether the clinic was targeted or destroyed accidentally, the effect was the same: to eliminate many of Falluja's doctors from the war zone. As Dr. Jumaili told the *Independent* on November 14: "There is not a single surgeon in Falluja." When fighting moved to Mosul, a similar tactic was used: on entering the city, U.S. and Iraqi forces immediately seized control of the al-Zaharawi hospital.

The images from the siege on Falluja came almost exclusively from reporters embedded with U.S. troops. This is because Arab journalists who had covered April's siege from the civilian perspective had effectively been eliminated. *Al-Jazeera* had no cameras on the ground because it has been banned from reporting in Iraq indefinitely. *Al-Arabiya* did have an unembedded reporter,

Abdel Kader Al-Saadi, in Falluja, but on November 11 U.S. forces arrested him and held him for the length of the siege. Reporters Without Borders and the International Federation of Journalists have condemned al-Saadi's detention.

"We cannot ignore the possibility that he is being intimidated for just trying to do his job," the IFJ stated.

It is not the first time journalists in Iraq have faced this kind of intimidation. When U.S. forces invaded Baghdad in April 2003, U.S. Central Command urged all unembedded journalists to leave the city. Some insisted on staying and at least three paid with their lives. On April 8, a U.S. aircraft bombed **al-Jazeera's** Baghdad offices, killing reporter Tareq Ayyoub. **Al-Jazeera** has documentation proving it gave the coordinates of its location to U.S. forces.

On the same day, a U.S. tank fired on the Palestine hotel, killing José Couso, of the Spanish network **Telecinco**, and Taras Protsiuk, of Reuters. The International Red Cross had tried to arrange a convoy out of Baghdad; inexplicably, it was reported that the Americans had refused it passage from the city.

At one point, Red Cross workers hoped to take the severely wounded Spanish television reporter with them – his leg had been amputated after the tank shell exploded below his office in the hotel – but he died during the afternoon. The American infantry divisional commander issued a statement that suggested the Reuters cameramen were sniping at the U.S. tank, a remark so extraordinary – and so untrue – that it brought worldwide protests from journalists. Three US soldiers are facing a criminal lawsuit from Couso's family, which alleges that U.S. forces were well aware that journalists were in the Palestine hotel and that they committed a war crime.

In Iraq, evidence is mounting that these voices are being systematically silenced through a variety of means, from mass arrests, to raids on hospitals, media bans, and overt and unexplained physical attacks. What is to stop the secret government from carrying this war of silence to the rest of the world?

Danny Casolaro

Danny Casolaro was a freelance journalist from Fairfax County, Virginia, who in 1991 was researching a book on the purported Justice Department theft of a proprietary software package called Prosecutor's Management Information System, or PROMIS for short.

PROMIS was developed by DC software firm Inslaw to help attorney's track caseloads. The Justice Department, however, reportedly found it well suited to track just about anyone and anything.

The PROMIS story led Casolaro to what he called **The Octopus**, a small group of individuals who were connected to some of the biggest scandals of the 1980s — the Savings & Loan collapse, Iran-Contra, and the 1980 October Surprise, in which aides for presidential candidate Ronald Reagan made a deal with Iranian guerillas to keep American hostages in captivity to prevent Jimmy Carter from winning the election. Ray Lavis, a computer specialist Casolaro had used as a source, told the **Washington Post** that Casolaro: "said he had narrowed the list of people to about 10," and that Casolaro thought "they were controlling the world."

On Thursday, August 8, 1991, Casolaro traveled to Martinsburg, West Virginia to meet with a source. He was confident that he was on the brink of a breakthrough, according to the *Village Voice*. But on Saturday, August 10, a housekeeper at the hotel where he had been staying found him in the bathtub, dead of an apparent suicide.

Casolaro's arms were slashed numerous times, and he was unclothed. On his bed lay a suicide note. All of his research documents were missing.

The Village Voice reported that, "In the weeks before his death Casolaro had spoken frequently about threats on his life, and just before he left for Martinsburg he had told his brother, 'If anything happens to me, don't believe it's an accident.'"

Officials ruled Casolaro's death a suicide. His body was embalmed before family members were notified or an autopsy performed, and his hotel room was thoroughly cleaned.

Casolaro's family maintained that he would not have committed suicide. They filed suit against the city of Martinsburg, West Virginia and other officials involved in the aftermath of his death. The suit was dismissed in September 1993.

According to Kenn Thomas, who has written what is no doubt the best book on the strange death of a journalist, *The Octopus: Secret Government and the Death of Danny Casolaro* (Feral House, 1996, 2004), Casolaro, like all great conspiracy writers, was dismissed as a paranoid crank. However, after his alleged suicide, no trace of his manuscript or accompanying notes has ever been found. So it seems that there is a conspiracy to hide information that Casolaro had uncovered. The question remains, what exactly did Casolaro discover that cost him his life?

An interesting development that has surfaced recently is the alleged use of the infamous Promis software by the secret government henchman Osama bin Laden. A Fox News report by correspondent Carl Cameron indicating that convicted spy, former FBI Agent Robert Hanssen, had provided the highly secret computer software program called Promis to Russian organized crime figures - who in turn reportedly sold it to Osama bin Laden.

Admissions by the FBI and Justice in the Fox story that they have discontinued use of the software are most certainly a legal disaster for a government that has been engaged in a 16-year battle with the software's creator, William Hamilton, CEO of the Inslaw Corporation. Over those 16 years, in response to lawsuits filed by Hamilton charging that the government had stolen the software from Inslaw, the FBI, the CIA and the Department of Justice have denied, in court and under oath, ever using the software.

Bin Laden's reported possession of Promis software was clearly reported in a June 15, 2001 story by *Washington Times* reporter Jerry Seper. That story went unnoticed by the major media.

In it Seper wrote, "The software delivered to the Russian handlers and later sent to bin Laden, according to sources, is believed to be an upgraded version of a program known as Promis - developed in the 1980s by a Washington firm, Inslaw, Inc., to give attorneys the ability to keep tabs on their caseloads. It would give bin Laden the ability to monitor U.S. efforts to track him down, federal law-enforcement officials say. It also gives him access to databases on specific targets of his choosing and the ability to monitor electronic-banking transactions, easing money-laundering operations for himself or others, according to sources."

In a series of stories by **The Times**, and as confirmed by parts of the Fox broadcast, it appears that Hanssen, in order to escape the death penalty, agreed to provide the FBI and other intelligence agencies with a full accounting of his sale of Promis overseas. Reports state that almost until the moment of his capture, Hanssen was charged with "repairing" and upgrading versions of the software used by Britain and Germany.

Two different spokespersons at the FBI's Office of Public Affairs said that: "The FBI has discontinued use of the Promis software." The spokespersons declined to give their names.

Department of Justice spokesperson Loren Pfeifle declined to answer any questions about where, when or how Promis had been used and would say only, "I can only confirm that the DoJ has discontinued use of the program."

Inslaw had two limited contracts to provide Promis to Justice in 1982 and 1983. Neither application had anything to do with tracking terrorist activities. Hamilton's suits charged that Reagan Administration officials, including Edwin Meese, pirated the software, modified it for intelligence and financial uses and made millions by selling it to the governments of Israel, Canada, Great Britain, Germany and other friendly nations. After the installation of a CIA-created "back door" into the program, Israel, using its lifelong Mossad agent Robert Maxwell, reportedly sold the software to "unfriendly" nations and then secretly retrieved priceless intelligence data.

The statements of FBI and Justice sources in the Fox story have made Hamilton's case. They also give but the barest hint of the security breaches that may now be helping the most wanted man in the world. Bin Laden's reported possession of Promis may also explain the alleged threatening messages that were received by President Bush while aboard Air Force One on 9/11.

A mild uproar erupted in the days after the WTC attacks when Presidential aide Carl Rove indicated that threatening calls had been placed to Air Force One just hours after the attacks while President Bush was onboard. Some journalists excoriated Rove for suggested that bin Laden might have a mole in the White House who could have given bin Laden the secure codes to reach the aircraft in flight.

Bin Laden's possession of Promis would provide a possible explanation. According to Hamilton, under the right circumstances, Promis could have enabled the threatening calls to be made.

"I have no way of knowing whether any Promis-related base has dial-up access to Air Force One. But if that happens, and if you have Promis, it's a straightforward thing to do. But one would still need to have access to the targeting computer. There is a central locator system to track members of the

National Command Authority 24/7. If that is a database created with Promis and if anyone had access you could do it."

Such a penetration using Promis might also explain why Vice President Dick Cheney was hurriedly whisked out of sight and reportedly taken to a secure underground facility, where he reportedly works to this day. Cheney's prolonged absences from the public eye would also be explained by such a breach of security.

Numerous news stories, books and investigative reports spanning nearly two decades, have established that Promis holds unique abilities to track terrorists. The software has also, according to numerous sources including Hamilton, been modified with artificial intelligence and developed in parallel for the world's banking systems to track money movements, stock trades and other financial dealings.

Systematics, since purchased by Alltel, an Arkansas financial and technical firm headed by billionaire Jackson Stephens, has often been reported as the primary developer of Promis for financial intelligence use. Systematics through its various evolutions had been a primary supplier of software used in inter-bank and international money transfers for many years. Attorneys who have been connected to Systematics and Promis include Webster Hubbell, Hillary Clinton and the late Vince Foster.

If true, and if claims by the FBI and the Department of Justice that they have "recently" discontinued the use of Promis are accurate, the likelihood than bin Laden may have compromised the systems the U.S. government and its allies use to track him is high. Additional information in the Fox broadcast indicating that Britain stopped using the software just three months ago and that Germany stopped using the software just weeks ago are equally disturbing.

These are mission-critical systems requiring years of development. What has replaced them? And even if the U.S. government has replaced the software given to its allies with newer programs - several of which FTW knows to be in existence - the Fox report clearly implies that bin Laden and Associates have had ample time to get highly secret intelligence data from both Britain and Germany. Those systems might, in turn, have compromised U.S. systems. The WTC attacks had - by all reckoning - been in the works for years, and bin Laden would certainly have known that the U.S. would be looking for him afterwards.

Approximately two weeks after the September 11 attacks on the World Trade Center and the Pentagon, the **History Channel** aired a documentary entitled, *The History of Terrorism*. In that documentary, a law enforcement officer described some of the methods used to track terrorist movements. He stated that "computers" were able to track such things as credit card purchases, entry and exits visas, telephone and utility usage etc. It was implied that these diverse data base files could be integrated into one unified table. He gave an example that through the use of such a system it would be possible to determine that if a suspected terrorist entered the country and was going to hide out, that by monitoring the water and electrical consumption of all possible suspects in a given cell, it would be possible to determine where the terrorist was hiding out by seeing whose utility use increased.

On the other hand, it would be possible to determine if a terrorist was on the move if his utility consumption declined or his local shopping patterns were interrupted. Aren't those "club" cards from your supermarket handy?

This is but the barest glimpse of what Promis can do. Combined with artificial intelligence, it is capable of analyzing not only an individual's, but also a community's entire life in real time. It is also capable of issuing warnings when irregularities appear and of predicting future movements based upon past behavior.

In the financial arena Promis is even more formidable. Not only is it capable of predicting movements in financial markets and tracking trades in real time. It has been reported, on a number of occasions, to be used, via the "back door" to enter secret bank accounts, including accounts in Switzerland and then remove the money in those accounts without being traced. Court documents filed in the various INSLAW trials include documentation of this ability as well as affidavits and declarations from Israeli intelligence officers and assets.

The one essential weakness of Promis is that it must be physically installed on a targeted computer for it to be effective. Hence, if Osama bin Laden is able to penetrate a U.S. Government system it must mean that Promis is there.

It has been reported that the CIA uses Promis to track stock trades in real time. Thus, as described in FTW stories on insider trading directly connected to the 9/11 attacks, the Agency had the ability to determine that immediate impending attacks were planned against both American and United Air Lines.

The Israeli Herzliyya Institute for Counterterrorism was able to publish a detailed accounting of the trades within days of the attacks and their report underscores the connection between counterterrorist efforts and the monitoring of financial markets. Suspicions of CIA advance knowledge of the attacks were heightened when FTW disclosed that the current Executive Director of the CIA, A.B. "Buzzy" Krongard was, until 1998, the CEO of A.B. Brown, the company which handled many of the suspicious trades.

A key question that remains is how many versions of the software had the CIA and the U.S. government given out and might they not have been also using a back door against "friendly" nations for economic motives to give advantage to U.S. companies? Fox news reported that Osama bin Laden once boasted that his youth "knew the wrinkles of the world's financial markets like the back of their hands and that his money would never be frozen."

The Bush family is connected to the bin Laden family through the Carlyle Group, which means that both the bin Laden fortune and the Bush fortune are greatly increased with every military act. If bin Laden is to remain armed and create worldwide fear to carry on the Bush agenda of turning America into a police state and leading us further into the New World Order, he needs further funding. With the Promise software, bin Laden need never worry again about how he will be funded.

Bank accounts can be very messy in that they can be traced, and indeed much U.S. money has already been traced to him and then quickly buried. Now bin Laden has the ability to create an account in any name to be collected whenever it is needed to obtain whatever is deemed necessary.

Paul Wilcher and the October Surprise

What makes the mysterious death of Paul Wilcher so disturbing is how little real attention has been paid to it. It seems that almost everyone has heard about Danny Casolero and the fact that his death was almost certainly a murder made to look like a suicide. Paul Wilcher, who was also investigating government conspiracies, died an equally suspicious death, yet this tragedy has almost disappeared into an information vacuum.

Wilcher was an attorney and had been investigating the claims of deep cover CIA operative Gunther Russbacher. Russbacher claimed to be the October Surprise pilot, who in 1980 flew George Bush to a secret meeting in France with Iranian officials. An agreement was made for Iran to delay the release of the 52 American hostages to ensure that Republican Presidential nominee, Ronald Reagan, would win the election over the incumbent Jimmy Carter.

Before his death, Wilcher had told friends and colleagues in Washington that he knew far more about the October Surprise and all the related scandals, such as the Inslaw scandal, the BCCI scandal and other government scandals and cover up's, than did Danny Casolaro. Wilcher's friend and colleague, Marion Kindig, said that Wilcher had expressed fear that he might be killed for "what he had in his head."

The last time Wilcher was seen by friends in the D.C. area was June 11, 1993. Because Wilcher was a regular guest of senior White House correspondent, Sara McClendon, she and Kindig became suspicious when he did not answer his phone or door. McClendon tried without success to get the D.C. police to open the door of his apartment. They appeared reluctant to get involved.

After numerous calls and pressure from McClendon, the police finally opened the door. Wilcher was found in his bathroom, sitting on the toilet. Cause of death was not determined.

McClendon and Kindig viewed the body to make identification. They were shown only the face, which was badly decomposed, swollen and purple. Both women said that the face looked as if it had been badly beaten. Neither woman, even though they knew Wilcher well, could make a positive identification.

Wilcher had been working on many different pieces of The Octopus at the time he was murdered. He had just asked Navy Intelligence operatives for a copy of the cockpit video from the SR 71 that Gunther had used to fly George Bush back from the October Surprise meeting in Paris. Since Bush was no longer President, it was felt that having the video would not cause Paul any problems.

According to the operatives who arranged for the delivery of the cockpit video, the drop was supposed to have occurred between June 10th and the 19th. Verification of its delivery was never confirmed. Mr. Wilcher was also in possession of documents showing the link between George Bush, Saddam Hussein and Bill Clinton in the BCCI-BNL bank scandals.

Wilcher had also been extensively briefed that the Branch Davidian compound in Waco, Texas was actually a CIA mind control operation that trained "sleeper" terrorists for future missions. David Koresh was a long time CIA asset and Waco had been a CIA center for mind control every since the end of World

War II. Many of the German mind control scientists were brought to Waco to continue their experiments.

Somehow the Waco "sleepers" had been triggered and was preparing to carry out their mission. Supposedly they were within days of finishing a nerve gas toxin that would have been powerful enough to kill up to 350 thousand people. Because of this, the government ordered that the compound be destroyed and everyone inside murdered.

According to Mr. Mason Lidell Jr., the superintendent of Wilcher's building, a Lieutenant and a Sergeant from the DC Police (with the help of firemen to force the door) entered Wilcher's apartment at about 11:30AM on June 23 1993. Three detectives from DC Police entered and found Wilcher's computer was turned on. When they read what was on the computer screen, they summoned the FBI. There is no further information on what the screen actually said.

After entering the apartment and getting a brief glance at the body and the apartment, Lidell was ordered to leave. The apartment was sealed off for the rest of the day, except for official personnel.

The body was removed at about 12:30 according to Lidell (who didn't witness this), though he did mention that when he entered the apartment later, there was blood on the floor and on the commode, which wasn't there before. He was told that this was because of measures taken to move the badly decomposed body.

At about 4:30 in the afternoon FBI Agents arrived. Sarah McClendon was also present, though not allowed in the apartment itself. She says two groups of four FBI Agents, eight FBI Agents in all, arrived and asked questions. McClendon checked their identification, which seemed convincing. According to Lidell at least three FBI Agents entered the apartment during the 4:30 to 7:30 time period.

Then, according to Lidell, one man appeared and said he was CIA (without offering identification). He joined the FBI agents in the Wilcher apartment during the 4:30 to 7:30 time period. More people could have entered during this time Lidell says: "he returned to his own apartment and didn't keep track."

Lidell says that an NBC camera crew was prevented from entering the apartment. Aside from firemen, medical personnel to remove the body and the above Government agents, no one was allowed in the apartment for the entire day - no reporters, friends, media crews, etc. This raises a question: why no other observers, since police okayed cleaning of the apartment the very next day?

Sara McClendon phoned the FBI to ask about the presence of FBI Agents, later Mr. James V. Desarno Jr., Assistant Special Agent in Charge from the DC Metropolitan Office, arrived. Mr. Desarno also asked questions, but strongly denied that the FBI was interested in or involved in the case. "We are not interested in this case," he told McClendon, Lidell and others repeatedly.

This seems curious. If Wilcher was a "nobody" why the official presence and vehement expression of non-involvement "ironic" with so many agents present? How could Desarno know the FBI would or wouldn't be involved without an investigation or known cause of death? Why all the secrecy and denial? Why the presence of the CIA?

The following is a message that Gunther Russbacher smuggled out of prison. The information had been given to him by some of the operatives who worked with him.

HOW PAUL WILCHER WAS MURDERED:

1. Paul was picked up at his apartment, taken to Vienna, VA where he was questioned as to the Bush, Webster and Carter account with London S.W. BCCI.

2. He was questioned for approximately 2 hours, at which time he was fed pizza. At 3:40 P.M. on the 18th of June, he was administered .025 mg of Curare via DSMO (as stabilizer). It was applied to the coating of the Pepsi bottle.

3. At point of death he was beaten to the face to make it look like a mugging. He was held in the trunk of a white and gray Ford Victoria (Maryland plates). He was taken to his apt. And as he was in rigor mortis, he was placed on the toilet. He emptied his bowels at death in another location. The bowel was removed and disappeared. Autopsy serology will show Curare/DMSO in the cardio vascular sack, (peridenum).

(The judge in Chicago died the same way Wilcher did. Judge Parsons was being primed and readied to accept a civil RICO filing. We were scheduled for filing 6-30-93. All documents have disappeared! Several others have died because of these issues.)

We were scheduled for filing 6-30-93. All documents have disappeared!! Several others have died because of these issues. Primary cause of death:

a. Bush/Russbacher video of the return flight from Paris in the SR-71.

b. Documents of BCCI and BNL moves.

c. Audio tapes of interviews by CIA covert operatives: 65 tapes, 92 hours.

d. WACO and the CIA, Delta Group involvement.

RENO IS IN ON ALL OF IT!

In a 1993 letter then Attorney General Janet Reno, Garby Leon of Columbia Pictures, and personal friend of Paul Wilcher, states: "A much larger issue is also implied here: if critics of our government are found dead in their bathrooms from obscure causes, and the government itself doesn't take steps to find out why, then our freedoms themselves are threatened--as well as the activities that protect those freedoms. If individual investigation and criticism of government activities is chilled or intimidated into silence, then democracy loses its most important protection.

"To put it another way, if Danny Casolaro's death was a message of some kind, then Wilcher's death is an even grimmer message--it suggests that Casolaro's death was not a fluke. Anyone inspired to follow Casolaro or Wilcher's path now has a strong added reason to fear doing so.

"And a real investigation into Wilcher's death might not be an academic exercise. One person who is extremely close to and knowledgeable about the Casolaro case has said in private that the mystery of Casolaro's death could be resolved by a Grand Jury investigation, with sworn testimony, subpoena power, etc. This suggests Paul Wilcher's death may not have to remain a mystery either."

Unfortunately, to this date, both Casolaro's and Wilcher's deaths remain a mystery.

Gary Webb and the CIA's Secret Cocaine Operation

In 1996, journalist Gary Webb wrote a series of articles for the ***San Jose Mercury News*** that forced an investigation into the Reagan-Bush administration's protection of cocaine traffickers who operated under the cover of the Nicaraguan contra war in the 1980s. Webb's articles, *Dark Alliance*, showed that the CIA planned and supported the importation of cocaine into the United States.

The *Dark Alliance* articles, while nothing new to those familiar with conspiracy theories, created an uproar, especially with the information that Nicaraguan drug traffickers had sold tons of crack cocaine from Colombian cartels in Los Angeles' black neighborhoods and then funneled millions in profits back to the CIA-supported Nicaraguan Contras. The ***San Jose Mercury News*** would later boast that: "It had published the first interactive expose in the history of American journalism."

While most of the nations major news organizations ignored Webb's expose, ***Dark Alliance*** took on a life of its own on the Internet. Subsequently, the fame of the Internet series forced the major newspapers to attack the reporter and eventually his own newspaper backed away from its support of Webb's series.

Mercury News editor Jerry Ceppos cowtowed to the big three, the ***New York Times***, the ***Washington Post*** and the ***Los Angeles Times***, and apologized for "shortcomings" in the series, not long after he had written that four ***Post*** reporters assigned to discredit the series "could not find a single significant error."

Despite the fact that Webb's articles were dismissed as "crackpot conspiracy theories," in 1998, in response to Webb's series, the CIA Inspector General admitted that the CIA was involved with the Contras, who were actively participating in cocaine trafficking. The Inspector General said more than 50

Contras and Contra units were implicated in the cocaine trade, that the CIA knew about it in real time, that it hid the evidence, and that it obstructed justice.

Despite these admissions, the **New York Times**, the **Washington Post**, and the **L.A. Times** still refused to deal with the facts. It seemed almost like the editors had more of a stake in covering up the truth than the CIA did. Gary Webb's career was allowed to be ruined and he was demoted Webb within the paper. He resigned and pushed his investigation even further in his book, **Dark Alliance: The CIA, the Contras, and the Crack Cocaine Explosion**.

The people who were involved in protecting the CIA from those major papers, their careers blossomed. Jerry Seapost, the executive editor of the **San Jose Mercury News**, who sold out Webb and his series, received an award from the Society of Professional Journalists for ethics because of what he did. So, it seemed like all of the people that did the wrong thing got the benefits, and Gary Webb and the people who did honorable work on this topic, received no benefits at all, and in fact were professionally damaged.

On December 10 2004, three employees of A Better Moving Company arrived at Webb's home in Carmichael, California with instructions to move the resident's belongings into storage. Webb had just sold the home for $321,750 and said that he would be moving in with his grandmother who lived nearby. When the men arrived at the door they found a handwritten note attached to the surface that read, "Please do not come in. Dial 911 and ask for an ambulance."

The moving men notified authorities with paramedics and the Sacramento Sheriff's Department arriving at 9:15AM. Inside they found the body of Gary Webb, dead from a several gunshot wounds to the head.

At 3:55 p.m. Friday afternoon Sacramento Coroner's Investigator Dave Brown determined that Gary Webb had committed suicide with a handgun. Dave Brown said that the first wound was not fatal and a second shot took the man's life. Dave Brown further stated, "There is no other possibility but suicide."

Spokesmen for the investigative units of three different sheriff's departments stated that suicides seen with two shots to the head inflicted by a handgun are extremely rare. Each man interviewed also said that they have heard of such cases but had never personally seen one.

The **Miami Herald** and **L.A. Times** continue to attack Webb even after his death in their obituaries. Both claimed that his work was discredited despite the fact that Webb was vindicated by congressional investigations.

After his death, it was revealed that Webb had been working on a new book detailing the Israeli secret service, MOSSAD, controlling drug trafficking in South America, all with the approval and help from the U.S. government. Webb was acutely aware that people get killed for revealing the kinds of horrors he uncovered. He was very concerned for the safety of his sources in prison and in Central America. The DEA raided the office of the literary agent who was helping him get a book contract. So Webb was aware of the possibility of being "suicided," and that he was concerned not just for himself, but also for his sources.

As well, shortly before he was found dead, Webb had told friends that he was under surveillance and that his phone and computer was being tapped.

Former DEA agent Cele Castillo concurs that Webb was murdered and that in such a "revenge hit" situation it was common in his experience that the murderers would have likely talked to Webb at length about how and why they were about to kill him.

There is also the strange fact that Webb's notes and manuscripts have turned up missing from his house. To this date, nothing has been found of Webb's extensive research material. Whatever secrets Webb was planning to uncover in his unpublished manuscript, has disappeared with him into the silence of the grave.

Robert Parry, who writes for **Consortium**, said in 1998 that new evidence, now in the public record, strongly suggests that the Reagan administration's tolerance of drug trafficking by the Nicaraguan contras and other clients in the 1980s was premeditated. With almost no notice in the national press, a 1982 letter was introduced into the Congressional Record revealing how CIA Director William J. Casey secretly engineered an exemption sparing the CIA from a legal requirement to report on drug smuggling by agency assets.

Attorney General William French Smith granted the exemption on Feb. 11, 1982, only two months after President Reagan authorized covert CIA support for the Nicaraguan contra army and some eight months before the first known documentary evidence revealing that the contras had started collaborating with drug traffickers.

The exemption suggests that the CIA's tolerance of illicit drug smuggling by its clients during the 1980s was official policy anticipated from the outset, not just an unintended consequence followed by an ad hoc cover up. The newly released letter, placed into the Congressional Record by Rep. Maxine Waters, D-Calif., on May 7, establishes that Casey foresaw the legal dilemma that the CIA would encounter should federal law require it to report on illicit narcotics smuggling by its agents. The narcotics exemption is especially noteworthy in contrast to the laundry list of crimes that the CIA was required to disclose.

Under Justice Department regulations, "reportable offenses" included assault, homicide, kidnapping, Neutrality Act violations, communication of classified data, illegal immigration, bribery, obstruction of justice, possession of explosives, election contributions, possession of firearms, illegal wiretapping, visa violations and perjury. Yet, despite reporting requirements for many less serious offenses, Casey fought a bureaucratic battle in early 1982 to exempt the CIA from, as Smith wrote: "the need to add narcotics violations to the list of reportable non-employee crimes."

The first publicly known case of contra cocaine shipments appeared in government files in an Oct. 22, 1982, cable from the CIA's Directorate of Operations. The cable passed on word that U.S. law enforcement agencies were aware of "links between (a U.S. religious organization) and two Nicaraguan counter-revolutionary groups [which] involve an exchange in (the United States) of narcotics for arms." The material in parentheses was inserted by the CIA as part of its declassification of the cable. The name of the religious group remains secret.

Over the next several years, the CIA learned of other suspected links between the contras and drug trafficking. In 1984, the CIA even intervened with the Justice Department to block a criminal investigation into a suspected contra role in a San Francisco-based drug ring, according to Hitz's report.

In December 1985, Brian Barger and Robert Parry wrote the first news article disclosing that virtually every Nicaraguan contra group had links to drug trafficking. In that Associated Press dispatch, they noted that the CIA knew of at least one case of cocaine profits filtering into the contra war effort, but that DEA officials in Washington claimed they had never been told of any contra tie-in. The Casey exemption explains why that was possible.

After the AP story ran, the Reagan administration attacked it as unfounded and the rest of the Washington press corps largely ignored the article. But it did help spark an investigation by Sen. John Kerry, D-Mass., who over the next two years amassed substantial evidence of cocaine smuggling in and around the contra war. Still, the Reagan and Bush administrations continued to disparage Kerry's probe and its many witnesses.

Through the end of the decade, the mainstream Washington media also denigrated the allegations. In April 1989, when Kerry released a lengthy report detailing multiple examples of how the contra war supplied cover for major drug trafficking operations, the nation's most prestigious newspapers – **The New York Times**, **The Washington Post** and the **Los Angeles Times** – published only brief, dismissive accounts.

The contra-cocaine issue arose again in 1996 with an investigative series by Gary Webb of the **San Jose Mercury-News**. Those stories traced how one of the contra drug conduits helped fuel the crack epidemic in Los Angeles. In response, the major newspapers again rallied to the CIA's defense. They denounced the series as overblown, although finally acknowledging that the allegations raised during the 1980s were true.

Hunter S. Thompson: Suicide or Murder?

Considering the way he lived his life, few were really surprised when gonzo author Hunter S. Thompson allegedly shot himself to death on February 20, 2005 at his Woody Creek, Colo., ranch. However, according to the March 4, 2005 issue of the **New York Post**, there are some serious irregularities surrounding the demise of Thompson, and local cops seemed to have done a lackluster job of investigating.

Police reports obtained by the **Rocky Mountain News** note that cops arriving on the scene heard shots being fired, that Thompson's son, Juan, was allowed to be alone with the body, and that there was something odd about the gun Thompson supposedly used to kill himself.

Before his death, Thompson seemed in good spirits and was not known to be depressed. And considering his long-winded style, the absence of a note seems strange - he'd typed only the single word "counselor."

There were no eyewitnesses to the shooting, only an "earwitness" - Thompson's wife, Anita, who was on the phone with him at the time and who later drank scotch with the corpse. Her account of the incident is inconsistent: She alternately has said that she heard a loud, muffled noise and that she heard nothing but clicking.

The behavior of Juan, who was in the house at the time of the shooting, also was unusual. Pitkin County Deputy Sheriff John Armstrong said that when investigators arrived on the scene they heard shots, but Juan assured them he had merely been firing off a salute to his dead dad. Investigator Joseph DiSalvo also let Juan enter the kitchen alone and drape a scarf over the body.

And in his report, Deputy Ron Ryan noted the semi-automatic Smith & Wesson 645 found next to Thompson's body was in an unusual condition. There was a spent shell casing, but although there were six bullets left in the gun's clip, there was no bullet in the firing chamber, as there should have been under normal circumstances.

DiSalvo said he did not check the gun, adding, "I think a bullet from the magazine should have cycled into the chamber" unless there was a "malfunction." A spent slug was found in the stove hood behind the body.

What is interesting is that Thompson had been working on a story about the World Trade Center attack at the time of his death. As Canada's **Globe and Mail** reported, Thompson had "stumbled across what he felt was hard evidence showing the towers had been brought down not by the airplanes that flew into them but by explosive charges set off in their foundations."

As well, Thompson was also allegedly working on a book detailing the infamous underground homosexual, pedophile, sex-ring that permeates the Republican elite in Washington, DC. The recent scandal of fake White House "reporter" Jeff Gannon AKA Gluckert, has uncovered previously unsuspected links with pedophile/kidnapping rings and evangelical churches that have moved into the Washington DC political arena.

This information was first released on Thursday, June 29 1989, on the front page of the **Washington Times** under the headline: *Homosexual prostitution Inquiry ensnares VIP's with Reagan, Bush. Call boys took midnight tour of White House'*

The story revealed the secret homosexual, pedophile parties that were being given to the political elite of Washington. In fact, teen-age prostitutes were being given midnight tours of the White House amidst cocaine-fuelled sex parties.

This story was beyond a doubt the biggest scandal of the 1980's that was completely obliterated by the Bush White House - A complete coordinated blackout by the ruling elite in cooperation with the American television networks. Most Americans have never heard of this explosive story, but not because people have not made an effort to publicly expose the scandal.

Former republican Senator John Decamp has worked tirelessly to get past the government controlled media by assisting in the production of the documentary: **Conspiracy of Silence** that was to air May 3, 1994 on the Discovery Channel. This documentary exposed a network of religious leaders and Washington politicians who flew children to Washington DC for sex orgies. As the story goes, at the last minute before airing, there was a massive effort from key Washington politicians who were implicated in the scandal to exert pressure on the channel to threatened the TV Cable industry with restrictive legislation if this documentary was aired.

Conspiracy of Silence was pulled before it aired and was subsequently "bought" by an unknown purchaser who had all copies destroyed. Fortunately, bootleg copies of the documentary have surfaced on the Internet, available for anyone who is interested in knowing just how corrupt the countries leaders actually are.

Unfortunately, more than a dozen people involved in the Franklin Case have died, violent, and mysterious deaths. It could be that Hunter S. Thompson, with his prestigious credentials, may have paid the ultimate price for delving too deeply into the new allegations of evangelical churches and televangelists being intimately involved in child kidnappings and prostitution rings in the United States.

It is fascinating considering the considerable political clout that certain right-wing evangelical church's and their leaders have enjoyed with the neoconservatives. It is highly likely that this clout has been paid-for with the supple, young bodies of innocents, cruelly given to grease the wheels of political favoritism.

Unfortunate Son: James Hatfield

James Hatfield was the author of *Fortunate Son: George W. Bush and the Making of an American President*. Hatfield's book caused a brief flap in the fall of 1999 when his publisher, St. Martin's Press, leaked a juicy tidbit to the news media: Fortunate Son contained allegations of an early-'70s Bush Junior cocaine arrest that had been scrubbed from official records, courtesy of George Bush senior's political connections.

Thanks to the controversy the leak created, *Fortunate Son* sold tens of thousands of copies after its release. But St. Martin's came under intense pressure from Bush lawyers, and subsequently pulled the remaining copies from bookstore shelves. In a remarkable echo of Soviet political culture, St. Martin's literally burned the unsold copies.

Fortunate Son was then picked up and republished by Soft Skull Press. The book's second edition, released in June 2001, revealed that one of Hatfield's main sources was none other than top Bush adviser, Karl Rove.

It is widely believed among Hatfield supporters that Rove intentionally chose Hatfield to be the cocaine-story messenger to ensure that what did happen, would: Hatfield himself became the excuse to brush aside *Fortunate Son's* cocaine allegations.

James Hatfield had a rather dubious history. He had been arrested in 1988 for hiring another person to plant a bomb in a former co-worker's car (some reports state that the intended target was a former boss). The bomb malfunctioned, however, and no one was injured. Hatfield was convicted and spent five years in prison. He later denied that he was the same person involved in the bomb plot when reporters confronted him about it in 1999.

It was Hatfield's own past that provided content for the avalanche of negative press following the book's release. As happened with Gary Webb, mainstream news outlets could not be bothered to investigate the allegations — they were too busy investigating Hatfield.

Hatfield also received death threats from one of the Bush allies who had confirmed Bush's cocaine arrest allegations. The threats named Hatfield's wife and daughter and said, "If you value their lives, you'd better back off." In early 2001, Hatfield accidentally found out his computer was bugged when he took it to be repaired. Could this mean that Bush strategists dug Hatfield's criminal record to discredit him and kill off his book?

In November 2001, Alternet.com reported, "In Hatfield's last interview, he reiterated his life was in danger: "They're gonna discredit me, or silence me the best way they can. I'm in a very vulnerable position. I've got two years left on parole, they could say 'we searched your house back in Arkansas and we found weed.' And that's all it takes.""

On Monday, July 16, 2001, approximately one month after Soft Skull re-released **Fortunate Son**, a warrant was issued for Hatfield's arrest in Benton County, Arkansas, where he lived. He was charged with financial identity fraud after allegedly attempting to obtain credit cards using a former colleague's name. On July 18, a housekeeper found his body lying in a bed at a Days Inn.

Officials ruled his death a suicide due to the farewell notes left for his wife, daughter and friends. In the notes, Hatfield blames alcohol, financial trouble, and the controversy surrounding **Fortunate Son** as reasons for his suicide. However, his wife has said that the notes were obvious forgeries and were not written by her late husband. Toxicology reports showed that Hatfield had overdosed on prescription medication and alcohol.

After Hatfield's death made the headlines, the official story force-fed to the corporate media that Hatfield was charged on July 17 with credit-card fraud. Police had confiscated his computer and given him 24 hours to turn himself in, but instead he checked into a motel, overdosed on prescription drugs and died.

However, why would a best-selling author try to commit credit-card fraud using a computer he believed was bugged? He was also afraid of breaking the terms of his parole, fearing that if he did, that he would be sent back to Texas to prison, where, he was convinced, he would be killed. In the police report, there's no mention of anything found in the computer that was confiscated, though it was the first item mentioned in the application for a search warrant.

CHAPTER SIX
Who Is Killing The World's Top Scientists?

More than 150 Iraqi scientists are thought to have perished at the hands of Israeli secret agents in Iraq since the fall of Baghdad to U.S. troops in April 2003, a seminar has found. The Iraqi ambassador in Cairo, Ahmad al-Iraqi, accused Israel of sending to Iraq immediately after the U.S. invasion "a commando unit" charged with the killing of Iraqi scientists.

"Israel has played a prominent role in liquidating Iraqi scientists. The campaign is part of a Zionist plan to kill Arab and Muslim scientists working in applied research which Israel sees as threatening its interests," al-Iraqi said.

According to U.S. officials, a senior Iraqi scientist who had been involved in Iraq's nuclear program was found murdered in Baghdad, possibly targeted by former members of Saddam Hussein's government. Iraqi aeronautical scientist, Muhyi Hussein Ali, was a professor at the College of Science at Baghdad University, was found dead in the Raghibah Khatun. He had been shot twice in the back.

The killing appears to be part of an effort to systematically eliminate Iraqi scientists and technicians involved in Saddam's nuclear program. The scientist had been involved in nuclear physics research, notably nuclear centrifugal force.

Although the reason for the assassination campaign is unclear, U.S. officials believe the killings represent an effort to conceal the scope of Iraq's nuclear program. Former CIA weapons inspector David Kay said that two Iraqi weapons scientists who had been cooperating with the U.S. military were shot, and one of them was killed. The murdered scientist was shot in the head outside of his apartment.

"We think it was because, in fact, he was engaged in discussions with us," Kay said. Iraqi scientists have been helping the Iraq Survey Group uncover the nuclear program, which had been on hold since 1991 with the goal of eventually being restarted.

Strange as it may seem, Iraqi scientists are not the only ones who apparently are being targeted for an untimely death. Since the 1980's, scientists involved in research and development of weapons, biology, and other disciplines have died mysteriously.

In 1983, President Reagan proposed a "Strategic Defense Initiative" to protect America and her allies with a high-tech shield against enemy nuclear missiles. His March, 23 speech envisions flocks of satellites that will shoot down incoming missiles with lasers, but projected costs of what Sen. Kennedy calls a "Star Wars" program are staggering, and since it will have to be virtually 100 percent effective, few scientists believe it is feasible at any cost. However, thanks to the allure of millions of dollars of top-secret, black budget money, dozens of defense contractors signed on to try and make Reagan's dream a reality.

Unfortunately, for some scientists, Reagan's dream soon became their worst nightmare. Between the years 1985 and 1988, over thirty scientists working for Marconi and Plessey Defence Systems in Great Britain died violent and highly unusual deaths.

The deaths were first brought to the American public's attention from an article written by Larry Wichman in the June, 1989 issue of **Hustler** magazine, (*Who's Killing the Star Wars Scientists?* - Volume 15, number 12). Wichman writes that each scientist was a skilled expert in computers, and each was working on a highly classified project for the Star Wars program. None had any apparent motive for killing himself.

The British government contends that the deaths are all a matter of coincidence. The British press blames stress. Others alluded to a fraud investigation involving the nation's leading defense contractor. Relatives left behind didn't know what to think.

One such strange suicide was that of Fifty-year-old Alistair Beckham, a successful British aerospace-projects engineer for Plessey LTD. His specialty was designing computer software for sophisticated naval defense systems. Like hundreds of other British scientists, he was working on a pilot program for the Strategic Defense Initiative.

In August 1988, after driving his wife to work, Beckham walked through his garden to a backyard tool shed and sat down on a box next to the door. He wrapped bare wires around his chest, attached them to an electrical outlet and stuffed a handkerchief in his mouth. He then pulled the switch, blasting electricity through his body. It was an extremely painful way to commit suicide, and highly unusual, as most people seek the least painful way to do themselves in.

Unlike the American public, the British were made aware of the unusual deaths as early as the fall of 1986. Within weeks of each other, two London-based Marconi scientists were found dead 100 miles away, in Bristol. Both were involved in creating the software for a huge, computerized Star Wars simulator, the hub of Marconi's SDI program. Both men had been working on the simulator just hours before their death. Like the others, neither had any apparent reason to commit suicide.

Vimal Dajibhai was a 24-year-old electronics graduate who worked at Marconi Underwater Systems in Croxley Green. In August 1986 his body was found lying on the pavement 240 feet below the Clifton Suspension Bridge in Bristol. An inquest was unable to determine whether Dajibhai had been pushed off the bridge or whether he had jumped. There had been no witnesses. The verdict was left open. Yet, authorities did their best to pin his death on suicide.

Police testified that Dajibhai had been suffering from depression, something his family and friends flatly denied, telling the press that Dajibhai had absolutely no history of personal or emotional problems.

Police also claimed that the deceased had been drinking with a friend, Heyat Shah, shortly before his death, and that a bottle of wine and two used paper cups had been found in his car. Yet, forensic tests were never done on the auto, and those who knew Vimal, including Shah, say that he had never taken a drink of alcohol in his life. Investigative journalists found discrepancies in other evidence. "A police report noted a puncture mark on Dajibhai's left buttock after his fall from the bridge," explains Tony Collins, who covered the story for Britain's **Computer News** magazine. "Apparently, this was the reason his funeral was halted seconds before the cremation was to take place."

Members of the family were told that the body was to be taken away for a second post-mortem, to be done by a top home-office pathologist. Then, a few months later, police held a press conference and announced that it hadn't been a puncture mark after all, that it was a wound caused by a bone fragment.

"I find it very difficult to reconcile the initial coroner's report with what the police were saying a few months later," Collins contends.

Officials didn't fare any better with the second Bristol fatality. Police virtually tripped over themselves to come up with a motive for the apparent, and unusually violent, suicide of Ashaad Sharif.

Sharif was a 26-year-old computer analyst who worked at the Marconi Defense Systems headquarters in Stanmore, Middlesex. On October 28, 1986, he allegedly drove to a public park not far from where Dajibhai had died. He tied one end of a nylon cord around a tree and tied the other end around his neck. Then he got back into his Audi 80 automatic, stepped on the gas and sped off, decapitating himself.

Marconi initially claimed Sharif was only a junior employee, and that he'd had nothing to do with Star Wars. Co-workers stated otherwise. At the time of his death, Sharif was apparently about to be promoted. Also, Ashaad reportedly worked for a time in Vimal Dajibhai's section.

The inquest determined that Sharif's death was a suicide. Investigating officers maintained that the man had killed himself because an alleged lover had jilted him. However, Ashaad hadn't seen the woman in more than three years.

"Sharif was said to have been depressed over a broken romance," Tony Collins explains. "But the woman police unofficially say was his lover contends that she was only his landlady when he was working for British Aerospace in Bristol. She's married, has three children, and she's deeply religious. The possibility of the two having an affair seems highly unlikely, especially since Sharif had a fiancée in Pakistan. His family told me that he was genuinely in love with her."

Police suddenly switched stories. They began to say that Sharif had been deeply in love with the woman he was engaged to, and that he'd decapitated himself because another woman was pressuring him to call off the marriage. Authorities claimed to have found a taped message in Sharif's car "tantamount" to a suicide note. On it, officers said, he'd admitted to having had an affair, thus bringing shame on his family. Family members who've heard the tape say that it actually gave no indication of why Sharif might want to kill himself. Sharif's family was told by the coroner that it was "not in their best interest" to attend the inquest.

"It's been almost impossible to get to information about the deaths that should be in the public domain," Tony Collins laments. "I've been given false names or incorrect spellings, or I've not been told where inquests have taken place. It's made it very difficult for me to try to track down the details in these cases."

In the Sharif case, two facts stand out: Family and friends all agree: Ashaad had no history of depression, and there was absolutely no reason for him to be in Bristol.

A widely held theory among the press is that the mysterious deaths could be the result of massive corruption at Marconi. According to a high-ranking British government official, the Ministry of Defense had been secretly investigating Marconi on allegation of defense-contract fraud, overcharging the government, and bribing officials.

The extensive probe reached as far as Marconi's subcontractors and into MoD research facilities such as the Royal Military College of Science and the Royal Air Force Research Center. Almost all of the dead scientists were associated with one or more of these establishments.

If Marconi was systematically defrauding the government for million off pounds each year, perhaps an employee stumbled upon incriminating evidence and had to be done away with. It would be easy enough to make it look like an accident.

Consider the odd death of Peter Peapell, found dead beneath his car in the garage of his Oxfordshire home. Peapell, 46, worked for the Royal Military College of Science, a world authority on communications technology, electronics surveillance and target detection. Peapell was an expert at using computer to process signals emitted by metals. His work reportedly included testing titanium for its resistance to explosives.

On February 22, 1987, Peapell spent the evening out with his wife, Maureen, and their friends. When they returned home, Maureen went straight to bed, leaving Peter to put the car away.

When Maureen woke up the next morning, she discovered that Peter had not come to bed. She went looking for him. When she reached the garage, she noticed that the door was closed. Yet she could hear the car's engine running.

She found her husband laying on his back beneath the car his mouth directly below the tail pipe. She pulled him into the open air, but he was already dead.

Initially, Maureen thought her husband's death an accident. She presumed he'd gotten under the car to investigate a knocking he'd heard driving home the night before, and that he'd gotten stuck. But the light fixture in the garage was broken, and Peter hadn't been carrying a flashlight.

Police had their own suspicions. A constable the same height and weight as Peter Peapell found it impossible to crawl under the car when the garage door was closed. He also found it impossible to close the door once he was under the car. Carbon deposits from the inside of the garage door showed that the engine had been running only a short time. Yet, Mrs. Peapell had found the body almost seven hours after she'd gone the bed.

The coroner's inquest could not determine whether the death was a homicide, a suicide or an accident. According to Maureen Peapell, Peter had no reason to kill himself. They had no martial or financial problems. Peter loved his job. He'd just received a sizable raise, and according to colleagues, he'd exhibited "absolutely no signs of stress."

Member of Parliament Douglas Hoyle, who issued a call for an official investigation into the strange string of deaths declared publicly that: "Something sinister appears to be going on."

"The number of these deaths is now becoming too odd to be a coincidence any more," he insisted.

The string of suspicious fatalities did not go unnoticed by the United States government. The American embassy in London publicly requested a full investigation by the British Ministry of Defense. According to Reagan Administration sources, "We cannot ignore it anymore."

The CIA suspected that the deaths were an indication of security leaks, that Star Wars secrets were being sold to the Russians. Perhaps these scientists had been blackmailed into supplying classified data to Moscow and could no longer live with themselves. One or more may have stumbled onto an espionage ring and been silenced. As NBC News London correspondent Henry Champ put it, "In the world of espionage, there is a saying: Twice is coincidence, but three times is enemy action."

The National Forum Foundation, a conservative Washington, D.C., think tank, believed that the deaths were the work of European-based, left wing terrorists, such as those who took credit for gunning down a West German bureaucrat who'd negotiated Star Wars contracts. The group also claims the July 1986 bombing death of a research director from the Siemens Company, a high-tech, West German electronics firm. They have yet to take credit for any of the scientists.

Another theory suggests that the Russians have developed an electromagnetic "death ray," with which they're driving the British scientists to suicide. The late conspiracy writer, Jim Keith, thought that this scenario was very likely due to the evidence that he had uncovered while researching an article on electromagnetic weapons.

Certainly this possibility has not been overlooked, as evidenced by the following quote from Zbigniew Brzezinski, in his book: ***Between Two Ages: America's Role in the Technetronic Era***: "It may be possible - and tempting - to exploit for strategic political purposed the fruits of research on the brain and on human behavior.

Gordon J.F. MacDonald, a geophysicist specializing in problems of warfare, has written that artificially excited electronic strokes could lead to a pattern of oscillations that produce relatively high power levels over certain regions of the earth. "In this way, one could develop a system that would seriously impair the brain performance of very large populations in selected regions over an extended period. No matter how deeply disturbing the thought of using the environment to manipulate behavior for national advantages to some, the technology permitting such use will very probably develop within the next few decades."

The Japanese conducted early electromagnetic weapons experiments during World War II. Information on these "death rays" was revealed when Japanese scientists were interrogated. According to reports of the scientists the death ray was never used on humans, but was tested on animals. In 1960 there were rumors of a fantastic new Soviet super weapon employing Nikola Tesla electromagnetic technology. With subsequent revelations about Soviet research in these areas, it seems that these rumors were true.

During the 1960s high levels of electromagnetic radiation were detected at the American embassy in Moscow. It was determined that the face of the embassy was being systematically swept with electromagnetic emissions by the Soviets. One guess was that a microwave beam was used to activate electronic equipment hidden within the building; another guess was more macabre: that the beam was being used to disrupt the nervous systems of American workers in the embassy.

Giving weight to the latter supposition, many of the employees of the embassy became ill. Ambassador Walter Stoessel suffered a rare blood disease likened to leukaemia, and experienced headaches and bleeding from the eyes. At least two other employees contracted cancer. According to researcher Alex Constantine, rather than informing embassy personnel of what was going on, the CIA chose to study the effects of the radiation.

Dr. Milton Zaret, called in to investigate what was termed "the Moscow Signal," reported that the CIA wondered, "whether I though the electromagnetic radiation beamed at the brain from a distance could affect the way a person might act," and, "could microwaves be used to facilitate brainwashing or to break down prisoners under investigation."

Zaret's conclusion about the Moscow Signal was that, "Whatever other reasons the Russians may have had, they believed the beam would modify the behavior of personnel."

Author Len Bracken, who was present in Moscow at the time, said that the microwave radiation was beamed from a shack on a building across from the embassy. In 1977 the microwave shack caught fire and burned. Bracken says, "It was a Friday night and the Marine House Bar was playing 'Burn, Baby, Burn' [i.e. "Disco Inferno"]." Bracken also relates that "in '79 a strange box was installed in the wall in my room [in Moscow], supposedly relating to the heating system."

Irradiation of the American embassy reportedly prompted a response from the Americans: the Defense Advanced Research Projects Agency's Project PANDORA, conducted at the Walter Reed Army Institute of Research from 1965 to 1970. One aspect of the project involved bombarding chimpanzees with microwave radiation. Referencing a reported statement by the head of the project, "the potential for exerting a degree of control on human behavior by low level microwave radiation seems to exist and he urged that the effects of microwaves be studied for possible weapons applications."

Within three years, Dr. Gordon J.F. McDonald, a scientific advisor to the president at the time, indicated that: "Perturbation of the environment can produce changes in behavioral patterns." The perturbation that McDonald was alluding to was EM waves, and the changes in behavior were altered brain wave patterns.

In 1965 the McFarlane Corporation in America came up with the Buck Rogers-sounding "modulated electron gun X-ray nuclear booster," a breakthrough in the "death ray" technology. Reports indicate that the device could also be used in communications, telemetry, and remote controlled guidance systems. McFarlane later claimed that NASA stole the system from him, and that the principles of the acknowledged death ray were employed in MIROS, what NASA described as an orbital "communications system."

Dr. Dietrich Beischer, a German scientist employed by the American government, irradiated 7,000 naval crewmen with potentially harmful levels of microwave energy at the naval Aerospace Research Laboratory in Pensacola, Florida, and talked about it at a symposium in 1973. Dr. Beischer disappeared soon after the experiment.

According to PANDORA alumnus Robert O. Becker, he was to spend some time with Beischer but, "Just before the meeting, I got a call from him. With no preamble or explanation, he blurted out: 'I'm at a pay phone. I can't talk long. They are watching me. I can't come to the meeting or ever communicate with you again. I'm sorry. You've been a good friend, goodbye.' Soon afterward I called his office at Pensacola and was told, 'I'm sorry, there is no one here by that name.' Just as in the movies. A guy who had done important research there for decades just disappeared."

According to Eldon Byrd, of the Naval Surface Weapons Center in Silver Springs, Maryland, "Between 1981 and September 1982, the Navy commissioned me to investigate the potential of developing electromagnetic devices that could be used as non-lethal weapons by the Marine Corps for the purpose of 'riot control,' hostage removal, embassy and ship security, clandestine operations, and so on."

Byrd wrote of experiments in irradiating animals with low level electromagnetic fields, mentioning changes in brain function, and stating that the animals "exhibited a drastic degradation of intelligence later in life... couldn't learn easy tasks... indicating a very definite and irreversible damage to the central nervous system of the fetus." The experiments went farther. Byrd wrote that, "At a certain frequency and power intensity, they could make the animal purr, lay down and roll over."

By the early 1970s, according to Robert C. Beck, "Anecdotal data amassed suggesting that a pocket-sized transmitter at power levels of under 100 milliwatts could drastically alter the moods of unsuspecting persons, and that vast geographical areas could be surreptitiously mood manipulated by invisible and remote transmissions of EM [electromagnetic] energy."

According to the **Oregon Journal**, in March 1978, in a story titled *Mysterious Radio Signals Causing Concern*, the city of Eugene was irradiated by microwaves possibly beamed from a Navy transmitter, located several hundred miles away in California. According to an FCC report, "microwaves were the likely cause of several sudden illnesses among faculty researchers at Oregon State University." Numerous residents also complained of headaches, insomnia, fatigue, skin redness, and hearing clicks and buzzes in the head.

A study conducted by the Pacific Northwest Center for Non-Ionizing Radiation attributed the radiation instead to the Soviets, stating that it was "psychoactive" and "very strongly suggesting of achieving the objective of brain control."

In September 1985, members of the Greenham Commons Women's Peace Camp in Great Britain, a global militarization protest camp located outside the U.S. Air Force Base at Greenham Commons, began experiencing a wide range of unpleasant physical symptoms including headache, depression, disorientation, memory loss, vertigo, and changes in their menstrual cycles. According to Dr. Rosalie Bertell and others who researched what was going on, the symptoms were of the type associated with exposure to radiation, and they began shortly after security at the base was switched from human guards to primarily electronic surveillance, this would have been a perfect opportunity to install electromagnetic broadcasting units disguised as surveillance equipment.

Dr. Bertell, former radar engineer Kim Besly, and others took readings of electromagnetic levels in the area, and found that they were as much as 100 times as strong as other nearby areas.

That the electromagnetic arsenal is being used against citizenry in the new Russia is quite apparent from a statement published at the end of 1991 by **SovData Dialine**:

"Psychological warfare is still being used by state security agents against people in Russia, even after the abortive August coup," said Emilia Chirkova, a Deputy of the Zelenograd Soviet and member of the Human Rights Commission. She recalls the scandal surrounding the alleged bugging equipment installed close to Boris Yeltsin's office. KGB agents admitted then that the directional aerial in the equipment was designed for transmission, not for reception. She believes it was part of an attempt to affect the health of the Russian president using high frequency electromagnetic radiation. "The Human Rights Committee," Chirkova said, "had warned Yeltsin about such a possibility."

Victor Sedleckij, design engineer-in-chief for the centre Forma and vice president of the League of Independent Soviet Scientists provide substantiation for Chirkova's allegations. Aedleckij stated, "As an expert... I declare, in Kiev was launched a mass production of psychotronic biogenerators and their tests. I cannot assert that during the [Moscow] coup d'etat those used were the Kiev generators... All the same, that [psychotronic generators] were used is evident to me. What are the psychotronic generators? They are electronic equipment that produces the effect of guided control in human organisms. It affects especially the left and right hemisphere of the cortex. This is also the technology of the U.S. Project Zombie 5... I draw on my personal experience since I am myself the designer of such a generator."

Emilia Chirkova cited several instances of the use of similar devices. Microwave equipment had been used in 1989 and 1990 in Vladivostok and Moscow prisons, in a mental hospital in Oryol, and in the Serbsky Institute in Moscow [also a mental hospital], she said. During his exile in Gorky, Andrei Sakharov noticed the presence of a high-tension electromagnetic field in his flat. It was reported recently in the press that Ruslan Khasbulatov, Speaker of the Russian Parliament, had to move from his flat to another district of Moscow. High-level electromagnetic radiation has been included among the possible causes of the discomfort he felt in his flat.

Purported victims of psychological warfare have written to the Russian paper. From Voronezh: "They controlled my laughter, my thoughts, and caused pain in various parts of my body... It all started in October 1985, after I had openly criticized the first secretary of the City Committee of the Communist Party."

"Sometimes voices can be heard in the head from the effect of microwave pulse radiation which causes acoustic oscillations in the brain", explained Gennady Shchelkunov, a radio electronics researcher from the Istok Association. In June 1991, a group of Zelenograd deputies sent an appeal signed by 150 people to President Yeltsin, demanding an investigation into the use of bio-electronic weapons.

An experiment conducted on CNN in the mid-1980s demonstrated the reality of electronic devices that can project images into the mind from a distance. Physicist Dr. Elizabeth Rausher and electrical engineer Bill VanBise built a radio frequency "mind interference machine" using information in the open Soviet scientific literature. According to CNN, "The machine was inexpensive and easy to construct using parts from a consumer electronics store. It emits a weak magnetic field pulsed at extremely low frequency."

Portable electronic mind control weapons, small enough to be transported by truck, are now reported to be used routinely in offensive actions by the American military, and were employed in Granada, Panama, the Gulf and Iraqi wars. It could be that the British scientists were targeted by such devices and somehow impelled to commit suicide. The big question is: who, or what was the perpetrator behind such actions?

Since that time, a number of researchers have taken it upon themselves to try and compile a list of SDI scientists who died less-than-natural deaths. Larry Wichman, at the end of his article offered up this list:

AUTO ACCIDENT—Professor Keith Bowden, 45, computer scientist, Essex University. In March 1982 Bowden's car plunged off a bridge, into an abandoned rail yard. His death was listed as an accident.

MISSING PERSON—Lieutenant Colonel Anthony Godley, 49, defense expert, head of work-study unit at the Royal Military College of Science. Godley disappeared in April 1983. His father bequeathed him more than 60,000 [pounds], with the proviso that he claims it by 1987. He never showed up and is presumed dead.

SHOTGUN BLAST—Roger Hill, 49, radar designer and draftsman, Marconi. In March 1985 Hill allegedly killed himself with a shotgun at the family home.

DEATH LEAP—Jonathan Walsh, 29, digital-communications expert assigned to British Telecom's secret Martlesham Heath research facility (and to GEC, Marconi's parent firm). In November 1985 Wash allegedly fell from his hotel room while working on a British Telecom project in Abidjan, Ivory Coast (Africa). He had expressed a fear for his life. Verdict: Still in question.

DEATH LEAP—Vimal Dajibhai, 24, computer-software engineer (worked on guidance system for Tigerfish torpedo), Marconi Underwater Systems. In August 1986 Dajibhai's crumpled remains were found 240 feet below the Clifton suspension bridge in Bristol. The death has not been listed as a suicide.

DECAPITATION—Ashaad Sharif, 26, computer analyst, Marconi Defense Systems. In October 1986, in Bristol, Sharif allegedly tied one end of a rope around a tree and the other end around his neck, and then drove off in his car at a high speed. Verdict: Suicide.

SUFFOCATION—Richard Pugh, computer consultant for the Ministry of Defense. In January 1987 Pugh was found dead, wrapped head-to-toe in rope that was tied four times around his neck. The coroner listed his death as an accident due to a sexual experiment gone awry.

ASPHYXIATION—John Brittan, Ministry of Defense tank batteries expert, Royal Military College of Science. In January 1987 Brittan was found dead in a parked car in his garage. The engine was still running. Verdict: Accidental death.

DRUG OVERDOSE—Victor Moore, 46, design engineer, Marconi Space Systems. In February 1987 Moore was found dead of a drug overdose. His death is listed as a suicide.

ASPHYXIATION—Peter Peapell, 46, scientist, Royal Military College of Science. In February 1987 Peapell was found dead beneath his car, his face near the tail pipe, in the garage of his Oxfordshire home. Death was due to carbon monoxide poisoning, although tests showed that the engine had been running only a short time. Foul play has not been ruled out.

ASPHYXIATION—Edwin Skeels, 43, engineer, Marconi. In February 1987 Skeels was found dead in his car, a victim of carbon monoxide poisoning. A hose led from the exhaust pipe. His death is listed as a suicide.

AUTO ACCIDENT—David Sands, satellite projects manager, Easams (a Marconi sister company). Although up for a promotion, in March 1987 Sands drove a car filled with gasoline cans into the brick wall of an abandoned cafe. He was killed instantly. Foul play has not been ruled out.

AUTO ACCIDENT—Stuart Gooding, 23, postgraduate research student, Royal Military College of Science. In April 1987 Gooding died in a mysterious car wreck in Cyprus while the College was holding military exercises on the island. Verdict: Accidental death.

AUTO ACCIDENT—George Kountis, experienced systems analyst at British Polytechnic. In April 1987 Kountis drowned after his BMW plunged into the Mersey River in Liverpool. His death is listed as a misadventure.

SUFFOCATION—Mark Wisner, 24, software engineer at Ministry of Defense experimental station for combat aircraft. In April 1987 Wisner was found dead in his home with a plastic bag over his head. At the inquest, his death was ruled an accident due to a sexual experiment gone awry.

AUTO ACCIDENT—Michael Baker, 22, digital-communications expert, Plessey Defense Systems. In May 1987 Baker's BMW crashed through a road barrier, killing the driver. Verdict: Misadventure.

HEART ATTACK—Frank Jennings, 60, electronic-weapons engineer for Plessey. In June 1987 Jennings allegedly dropped dead of a heart attack. No inquest was held.

DEATH LEAP—Russel Smith, 23, lab technician at the Atomic Energy Establishment. In January 1988 Smith's mangled body was found halfway down a cliff in Cornwass. Verdict: Suicide.

ASPHYXIATION—Trevor Knight, 52, computer engineer, Marconi Space and Defense Systems. In March 1988 Knight was found dead in his car, asphyxiated by fumes from a hose attached to the tail pipe. The death was ruled a suicide.

ELECTROCUTION—John Ferry, 60, assistant marketing director for Marconi. In August 1988 Ferry was found dead in a company-owned apartment, the stripped leads of an electrical cord in his mouth. Foul play has not been ruled out.

ELECTROCUTION—Alistair Beckham, 50, software engineer, Plessey. In August 1988 Beckham's lifeless body was found in the garden shed behind his house. Bare wires, which ran to a live main, were wrapped around his chest. No suicide note was found, and police have not ruled out foul play.

ASPHYXIATION—Andrew Hall, 33, engineering manager, British Aerospace. In September 1988 Hall was found dead in his car, asphyxiated by fumes from a hose that was attached to the tail pipe. Friends said he was well liked, had everything to live for. Verdict: Suicide.

Raymond A. Robinson added these names to the list in, ***The Alien Intent (A Dire Warning)***:

Shani Warren, twenty-six years old. Personal assistant in a company called Micro Scope, which was taken over by GEC Marconi less than four weeks after her death. Found drowned in 45cm. (18in) of water, not far from the site of David Greenhalgh's death fall. Warren died exactly one week after the death of Stuart Gooding and serious injury to Greenhalgh on April 10, 1987. She was found gagged with a noose around her neck. Her feet were also bound and her hands tied behind her back. Coroner's verdict: Open. (It was said that Warren had gagged herself, tied her feet with rope, then tied her hands behind her back and hobbled to the lake on stiletto heels to drown herself.)

David Greenhalgh, forty-six years old. NATO Defense Contracts Manager with ICL, who was working on the same defense project as David Sands. Mysterious 12m (40ft.) leap from a bridge at Maidenhead, Berkshire, on April 10 1987, the same day as Stuart Gooding's fatal car crash. He survived the fall and confirmed that he had no idea of how he had leapt from the bridge.

Avtar Singh Gida, twenty-seven years old. Belonged to the MOD Admiralty Research Establishment. Disappeared mysteriously in January 1987 while writing his doctoral thesis on underwater signal processing at Loughborough University. Both mainland police and Interpol launched searches for him in several countries, without success. He eventually reappeared four months later. He had been traced to a red light district of Paris and confirmed that he did not know precisely how he had got there. Allegedly, he has returned to his work and has said he does not want to discuss his disappearance or the death of his colleague, Vimal Dajibhai.

Then there is the unusual death of British defense journalist Jonathan Moyle, who was found hanged in his Santiago, Chile hotel room on April 1 1990. Both the sequence of events that may have led to his death and the exact circumstances of how Moyle died are shrouded in mystery and suspicion.

In March 1990, Moyle attended the Chilean Arms Fair in his capacity as editor of **Helicopter Defence World** as the Pinochet dictatorship drew to an end and Iraq prepared to invade Kuwait, precipitating the Gulf conflict. Weeks later he was dead. The coroner at first ruled a verdict of suicide, later changed to murder.

The cause of death was concluded to be asphyxiation but here there is a major discrepancy. Moyle was 5 feet 8 inches tall but the rail in the closet from which he was suspended was only five feet high. An autopsy revealed sedative in his stomach and a bruise on his leg.

The fact that no one has been charged with his murder has led to speculation that he intended to make startling revelations about the nature of the British-Iraq arms trade by others in the international defense circle in which he had moved. Moyle read **International Politics** at Aberystwyth on an RAF scholarship in 1980. It is alleged that as a bright student, Moyle was recruited at University into MI6 by his personal tutor and head of department, John Garnett, to work as a local special branch informant.

From here on Moyle immersed himself into a world of high-level military access, trusted by the Ministry of Defence to view classified documents and enjoying operational contact with the American drugs Enforcement Agency. He had clearly amassed considerable knowledge of the machinations of arms trafficking conducted between industrialized nations and the Third World by the time he came to cover the Chilean Air Fair.

The Fair is Latin America's most impressive display of military hardware and it seems inconceivable given his history, that Moyle was not approached by a government agency to gather intelligence on who was in attendance. Moyle had a friend from university, Catherine Royal, at the British Embassy in Santiago. However, shortly after his death both the resident air and naval attachés there returned to London along with royal and the first secretary was transferred.

What did Jonathan Moyle know or was about to discover that got him killed? On the night of his death Moyle was seen arguing with a man identified as Raul Monteciros, the public relations officer to the immensely influential Chilean arms dealer Carlos Cardoen, an associate of Mark Thatcher, son of former British Prime Minister, Margaret Thatcher.

Cardoen was using Chile as a conduit to get the arms to Iraq that Britain was secretly supplying to Saddam Hussein, namely re-exporting prohibited weapons including equipment supplied by Matrix Churchill Ltd., the British tool-maker whose Chairman was Iraq's procurement leader, Safa al Habobi. Perhaps key to the puzzle of Jonathan Moyle's death is the Marconi **Stonefish** smart mine. It seems possible Cardoen had secretly acquired the plans to the anti-ship mine (used by NATO forces) and had manufactured a sizeable quantity to be exported to Iraq. Iraq's rejuvenated underwater defense system would consequently pose a real hazard to American warships patrolling in the Gulf.

Moyle's father, Tony, was visited by Naval Intelligence officials five days after his son's death, asking if Jonathan had ever mentioned **Stonefish**. Shortly after, a smear story apparently with its origins in the Foreign Office, was circulated suggesting that Moyle's death was not an assassination but a self-inflicted consequence of a sadomasochistic sexual act. No evidence was given to support this theory and Tony Moyle later received a written apology from the Foreign Office.

To date there has been no comprehensive investigation of the Moyle murder case, either by the British government or the Chilean authorities. It seems most likely he was killed by the CNI - the Chilean Paramilitary Secret Police Force - better know by its previous initials, DINA. It appears equally likely, with Chile on the eve of parliamentary rule in 1990, that CNI's deadly efficient skills would only have been used with at least a wink of complicity from either the Chilean authorities or the Thatcher government, or both.

The arrest of General Pinochet in October has upset many in the British corporate military sector. The ex-dictator had been invited here as a guest of the Ministry of Defence and saw his role as an arms procurer for the Chilean army, though this was not Pinochet's official capacity.

It appears the Chilean navy will not now spend £60 million plus on purchasing new frigates from Britain and that BAE System's bid for refurbishing the Chilean air force with the Gripen fighter plane will probably lose out to American F-15 Tomcats. As with the cases of the two British nationals, Michael Woodward, an Anglo-Chilean priest, and William Beausire, a British businessman - who were tortured and murdered under General Pinochet's regime in Chile in the 1970s - which were deemed "insufficient" to arrest the former dictator, so the sacrifice of Jonathan Moyle is discreetly forgotten in the presence of large arms contracts.

Dead Microbiologists: 9/11 and the Anthrax Letters

After the terrorist attacks on September 11, 2001, a jittery United States was suddenly faced with what seemed to be a new series of terrorist campaigns in the form of letters that contained deadly anthrax spores. The first letters were sent to media outlets like the New York Post, American Media in Florida, NBC's Tom Brokaw, and at the New York offices of CBS and ABC. Letters were also sent to Democratic Senators Tom Daschle and Patrick Leahy in Washington DC.

Overall, twenty-three people contracted anthrax from these letters, and five died as a result from the exposure. Of the people who contracted anthrax, 11 worked for the postal service and eight for media organizations. (An infant who visited her mother at ABC News in New York also fell ill.) But three other people—a bookkeeper in New Jersey, a nurse in New York City, and an elderly widow in rural Connecticut—also caught anthrax, and the last two died.

The letters that were recovered by the FBI made references to "Death to America" and "Death to Israel," and gave the appearance of being written by Arab terrorists. However, discrepancies such as the date being written in the "month first" style used predominately in the U.S. (09-11-01), rather than the "day-first" style used by Islamic countries (11-9-01), convinced investigators early-on that the letter writer was more than likely from the United States. It is also interesting to note that the only U.S. politicians to receive the deadly letters were prominent Democrats who were opposing President Bush's new "anti-terror" policies.

Congress got their Anthrax letters just in time for the vote on the disingenuously named Patriot Act (aka the anti-terror bill) which the terrorized Senators voted into law, even though they were not given any time to read what they were voting on. The country was under attack once again. According to the Bush administration you either had to agree completely with the new draconian laws they were trying to pass, or you were unpatriotic, and possibly even treasonous.

The anthrax letters couldn't have come at a better time for those officials who had been wanting to make changes in the Constitution and Bill-of-Rights. Many politicians felt that U.S. citizens had far too many freedoms that could cause dissent against elected officials who were seen as increasingly corrupt and immoral. With the anthrax letters coming so soon after the deadly attacks of 9/11, the citizenry of the U.S. were more-than-willing to give up their rights and freedoms in exchange for guarantees of safety from foreign terrorists.

When investigators began to closely analyze the letters and the white powder they contained, they made some shocking discoveries. When U.S. Army experts gathered around a microscope in a specially sealed room to examine the anthrax spores that had been mailed to Sen. Thomas A. Daschle, the tiny spores, each one less than one-twentieth the diameter of a human hair, kept leaping off the glass microscope slide as though by magic, then wafting away like weightless wisps of cigarette smoke.

When the scientists tried to weigh the sample, the spores refused to rest on the scale but again became airborne, propelled by imperceptible air movements and tabletop vibrations. Finally the team dunked some of the spores in liquid chemicals and embedded others in wax just so they could examine and test them. That prevented further losses, but even then investigators ran short of spores long before they had done every test they had hoped to do.

A battery of biological assays followed. Tests for antibiotic sensitivity indicated the bugs were not resistant to standard antibiotics. DNA tests confirmed they belonged to the Ames strain, as have all of the terrorism-related specimens. And electron microscope studies of the powder in paraffin showed that the particles were remarkably small -- just 1.5 to 3 microns in diameter -- and consisted almost entirely of purified spores, a perfect recipe for inhalational anthrax. This meant that the anthrax used in the letters sent to both Sen. Daschle and Leahy were meant to escape the envelopes when opened and inhaled, as inhaling anthrax is potentially much more deadly.

But there was something else in there, too, and it would require analysis by others to say what. That job fell to a laboratory on the campus of the Armed Forces Institute of Pathology in Northwest Washington. An aging building there is home to a device called an energy dispersive X-ray spectroscope, which can detect the presence of extremely tiny quantities of chemicals.

That device found that silica, but not aluminum, was mixed with the Daschle spores – an important finding that differentiated the sample from known Iraqi specimens in which spores were combined with bentonite, a mixture of silica and aluminum. The spectroscope found traces of other elements, too, but there was virtually no specimen left for follow-up studies.

The Leahy letter contained enough refined anthrax spores to kill over 100,000 people. The Daschle letter probably had an equal amount. According to The *New York Times*, the anthrax in the Leahy letter officially weighed just 0.871 grams. And the other letters had roughly the same amount. (There are numerous articles that incorrectly say there were about two grams in each letter.)

All the anthrax found in the letters is now known to be from the "Ames strain," which originated in Texas and was sent to the U.S. Army for research in 1980. The Army later distributed it to various academic institutions for study. Since that time the strain has been further widely distributed to researchers around the world. A DNA analysis shows that the anthrax originated at the USAMRIID facility in Fort Detrick, MD. While other government laboratories obtained Ames anthrax from Ft. Detrick, the number of such labs is not very large.

It is important to note that the FBI has stated, "The anthrax utilized in (the Daschle letter) was much more refined, more potent, and more easily disbursed than letters to the *New York Post* and NBC." Later information indicated that the anthrax in the letters to the two Senators was ten times as pure as the anthrax in the letters to the media. It is very obvious that the "weponized" anthrax sent to the Democratic Senators was meant not to scare them, but to kill them. Their deaths were meant to scare the rest of the Democratic opposition from standing in the way of the Bush administration bulldozer.

Even though thousands of man-hours have been spent in the anthrax investigations, no arrests were ever made. Several people of "interest" have emerged, all with extensive connections with the military and bio-warfare research. Allegations have been made that the FBI knows who is responsible for the anthrax attacks, but due to the perpetrators connections with extreme right-wing factions, the military and possibly even the White House, this information has been withheld from the public.

One sinister outcome of the anthrax mailings has been the persecution of microbiologists in the United States. Several scientists have been arrested and jailed on trumped up charges, while others have met even more disturbing fates. The speculation is that the same domestic terrorists responsible for the anthrax letters are planning more biological attacks within the United States, and microbiologists would be the first wave brought in to fight such an attack. It is obvious that if leading scientists and microbiologists are dead or incapacitated, there is no hope in battling the deadly attacks.

In the *Complete 911 Timeline*, an open-content project managed by Paul Thompson, several incidents occurred prior to 9/11 that suggested the development of a domestic terrorist plot using anthrax and blaming Arab terrorists. On April 24 1997, a package containing a petri dish mislabeled "anthracks" is received at the B'nai B'rith headquarters in Washington, DC. The choice of B'nai B'rith probably was meant to suggest Arab terrorists, because the building had once been the target of an assault by Muslim gunmen.

The dish did not contain anthrax but did contain bacillus cereus, a very close, non-toxic cousin of anthrax used by the U.S. Defense Department. There are similarities to the later real anthrax attacks such as the misspelling "penacilin." In July 2002, B'nai B'rith claims the FBI still hasn't asked them about this hoax anthrax attack.

In February 1999, there is another hoax anthrax attack. A handful of envelopes with almost identical messages are sent to a combination of media and government targets including the **Washington Post**, NBC's Atlanta office, a post office in Columbus, Georgia (next to Fort Benning, an Army base), and the Old Executive Office Building in Washington. The letters contained fake anthrax powder. What makes this interesting is as of 1997, U.S. bio-defense scientists were working basically only with wet anthrax, while by 1999 some had experimented with making powders." The **New York Times** later suggests that scientist Steven Hatfill could have been behind this attack and the one in 1997. Could there be a connection between this hoax and a classified CIA report about sending anthrax through the mail released the same month?

The classified report discusses responses to an anthrax attack through the mail. The report, precipitated by a series of false anthrax mailings, is written by William Patrick, inventor of the U.S. anthrax weaponization process, under a CIA contract. Steven Hatfill commissioned the report, a good friend of Patrick. The report describes what the U.S. military could do and what a terrorist might be able to achieve.

The similarities between what the report predicted and the anthrax attacks that eventually happen after 9/11 are startling. The BBC later suggests the "possibility that there was a secret CIA project to investigate methods of sending anthrax through the mail which went madly out of control" and that the anthrax attacker knew of this study or took part in it. The CIA and William Patrick deny the existence of this report, even though copies have been leaked to the media.

On October 2 2001, days before the anthrax attacks begin, a strange letter is sent to a researcher in Fort Detrick, Maryland (USAMRIID). The letter is addressed to Dr. Ayaad Assaad, a Muslim anthrax researcher who was born in Egypt. The unsigned letter calls Assaad a "potential terrorist," with a grudge against the United States and the knowledge to wage biological warfare against his adopted country.

This is the latest in a series of attacks against Assaad, which include anonymous long hateful poems about him in the early 1990s. Assaad was laid off in 1997. The author of the letter says he is a former colleague of Assaad. The letter seems like a not-very-subtle attempt to frame Assaad for the anthrax attacks about to come. The letter strongly suggests the attacks could have been by someone at USAMRIID with a long time grudge against Assaad. Anthrax suspect Philip Zack later emerges as one (but not the only) coworker with such a grudge.

On November 12 2001, Dr. Benito Que, 52, was found murdered. An expert in infectious diseases and cellular biology at the Miami Medical School, Dr. Que was suspected by the to have been beaten on November 12 in a carjacking in the medical school's parking lot. Strangely enough, though, his body showed no signs of a beating. Doctors then began to suspect a stroke, but no evidence of a stroke was found.

On November 16 2001, Dr. Don Wiley, 57, disappears during a business trip to Memphis, Tennessee. He had just bought tickets to take his son to

Graceland the following day. Police found his rental car on a bridge outside Memphis. His body was later found in the Mississippi River. Forensic experts said he may have had a dizzy spell and fallen off the bridge. Police will only say, "We began this investigation as a missing person investigation. From there it went to a more criminal bent."

Wiley is seen as one of the world's leading researchers of deadly viruses, including HIV and the Ebola virus. Wiley worked at the Howard Hughes Medical Institute at Harvard University, and was an expert on the immune system's response to viral attacks. He was widely regarded as the nation's foremost expert in using special X-ray cameras and mathematical formulas to make high-resolution images of viruses. The FBI allegedly monitored the investigation because of Wiley's research knowledge.

A few days later, on November 21 2001, world-class microbiologist and high-profile Russian defector Dr. Vladimir Pasechnik, 64, dies of a stroke. Pasechnik, who defected to Britain in 1989, had played a huge role in the development of Russian biowarfare, heading a lab of 400 with an unlimited budget and the best staff available. He said he was successful in producing an aerosolized plague microbe that could survive outside the laboratory.

Pasechnik was connected to Britain's spy agency and recently had started his own company. In the last few weeks of his life he had put his research on anthrax at the disposal of the British government, in the light of the threat from bioterrorism.

Three more microbiologists were killed on November 24 2001, when a Swissair flight from Berlin to Zurich crashes during its landing approach; 22 passengers are killed and nine survive. Among those killed are Dr. Yaakov Matzner, 54, dean of the Hebrew University school of medicine; Amiramp Eldor, 59, head of the haematology department at Ichilov Hospital in Tel Aviv and a world-recognized expert in blood clotting; and Avishai Berkman, 50, director of the Tel Aviv public health department and businessman.

In a highly publicized murder, on December 10 2001, Dr. Robert Schwartz, 57, was stabbed and slashed with what police believe was a sword in his farmhouse in Leesberg, Virginia. His daughter, who identifies herself as a pagan high priestess, and three of her fellow pagans were charged. All were part of what they called a coven, and interested in magic, fantasy and self-mutilation. The police had no motive as to why they would have wanted to kill Schwartz, who was a single parent and said to be very close to his children. Schwartz worked at Virginia's Center for Innovative Technology on DNA sequencing and pathogenic microorganisms.

Four days later on December 14 2001, Nguyen Van Set, 44, died in an airlock filled with nitrogen in his lab in Geelong, Australia. The lab had just been written up in the journal *Nature* for its work in genetic manipulation and DNA sequencing. Scientists there had created a virulent form of mousepox. "They realized that if similar genetic manipulation was carried out on smallpox, an unstoppable killer could be unleashed," according to *Nature*.

In January 2002, the newspaper *Pravda* reports that Ivan Glebov and Alexi Brushlinski, two prominent Russian microbiologists who were well known

119

around the world and members of the Russian Academy of Science, died as the result of a bandit attack in Moscow.

On February 9 2002, Victor Korshunov, 56, is attacked, struck over the head and killed at the entrance of his home in Moscow, Russia. He was the head of the microbiology sub-faculty at the Russian State Medical University and an expert in intestinal bacteria.

Two days later on February 11 2002, Dr. Ian Langford, 40, was found dead, partially naked and wedged under a chair in his home in Norwich, England. When found, his house was described as "blood-spattered and apparently ransacked."

Langford was an expert in environmental risks and disease and a senior Fellow at the University of East Anglia's Centre for Social and Economic Research on the Global Environment. One of his colleagues states: "Ian was without doubt one of Europe's leading experts on environmental risk, specializing in links between human health and environmental risk... He was one of the most brilliant colleagues I have ever had."

That same month on February 28 2002, in San Francisco while taking delivery of a pizza, Tanya Holzmayer, 46, is shot and killed by a colleague, Guyang Huang, 38, who then apparently shot himself. Holzmayer moved to the U.S. from Russia in 1989. Her research focused on the part of the human molecular structure that could be affected best by medicine. Holzmayer was focusing on helping create new drugs that interfere with replication of the virus that causes AIDS. One year earlier, Holzmayer obeyed senior management orders to fire Huang.

On March 24 2002, David Wynn-Williams, 55, is hit by a car while jogging near his home in Cambridge, England. He was an astrobiologist with the Antarctic Astrobiology Project and the NASA Ames Research Center. He was studying the capability of microbes to adapt to environmental extremes, including the bombardment of ultraviolet rays and global warming.

The next day on March 25 2002, Steven Mostow, 63, died when the airplane he was piloting crashes near Denver, Colorado. He worked at the Colorado Health Sciences Center and was known as "Dr. Flu" for his expertise in treating influenza, and expertise on bioterrorism. Mostow was "one of the country's leading infectious disease experts" and was associate dean at the University of Colorado Health Sciences Center. Three others died in the crash. Mostow's death brings the total number of leading microbiologists killed in a six-month period to at least 15.

On June 1 2002, in Memphis, Tennessee, medical examiner O.C. Smith is attacked with a chemical spray, bound with barbed wire, and left lying in a nearby parking lot with a bomb tied to his body. He is rescued several hours later.

In recent months, Smith has been working on two interesting cases. One is the death of Harvard University microbiologist Don Wiley, who supposedly fell from a Memphis bridge. He also helped identify the body of Katherine Smith, a state driver's license examiner who was found burned beyond recognition in February 2002, a day before a hearing on federal charges of helping five Middle Eastern men obtain fake driver's licenses. Adding to the mystery, Smith had received a series of death threat letters early in 2001. Perhaps it's all coincidence, but the events around O.C. Smith, Katherine Smith and Don Wiley seem to tie 9/11 and the rash of microbiologist deaths together in some inexplicable way. If someone wanted O.C. Smith dead, why didn't they just kill him instead of attacking him in such a strange way and then leaving him to live? Was this, and an earlier bomb attack against his office meant as a warning?

October 11, 2003: West Nile researcher, Dr. Michael Perich, 46, died in a one-vehicle car accident. Perich crashed his Ford pickup truck when, for unknown reasons, it veered off the highway about three miles east of Walker, Louisiana, flipped and landed in rainwater. Perich, who was wearing his seat belt, drowned. From 1986 to 1992, Perich worked at Fort Detrick in Frederick, Md., as the vector suppression program manager and research medical entomologist. The anthrax used in the U.S. attacks is now known to have originated at Fort Detrick.

November 2, 2003: Vladimir Pasechnik defected from the Former Soviet Union to Great Britain while on a trip to Paris. He had been the top scientist in the USSR bioweapons program, which is heavily dependent upon DNA sequencing. In the last few weeks of his life he had put his research on anthrax at the disposal of the British and U.S. governments, in the light of the threat from bioterrorism. The cause of the death was certified as a stroke. But it has emerged that a pathologist attached to MI5, Britain's internal security service, examined the body. His findings are not known. "There are a number of nerve agents that can mimic a stroke and leave no traces," said Dr. Leonard Horowitz, a U.S. specialist in the field of toxic poisons.

November 20, 2003: Robert Leslie Burghoff, 45, a postdoctoral fellow at Baylor College of Medicine's molecular virology and microbiology department in Houston, was studying the virus that was plaguing cruise ships until he was killed while he was walking to his car. Burghoff was hit from behind by a mysterious white or light-colored cargo van that jumped the sidewalk. He was killed instantly. There have been no arrests and no suspects.

January 6, 2004: Dr. Richard Stevens, 54, Hematologist. Disappeared after arriving for work on July 21, 2003. Steven's disappearance sparked a national manhunt and he allegedly killed himself because he could not cope with the stress of a secret affair, a coroner has ruled.

March 11, 2004: Vadake Srinivasan, originally from India, was one of the most-accomplished and respected industrial biologists in academia, and held two doctorate degrees. He died in a mysterious single car accident in Baton Rouge, Louisiana.

May 14, 2004: Dr. Eugene F. Mallove, 56, died after being beaten to death during an alleged robbery. Dr. Mallove had a broad experience in high technology engineering for government agencies and the military at companies including Hughes Research Laboratories and MIT.

June 16, 2004: William T. McGuire, 39, of Woodbridge, New Jersey. His dismembered body was found floating in three suitcases in the Chesapeake Bay. McGuire was a senior programmer analyst and adjunct professor at the New Jersey Institute of Technology in Newark.

Strange and Unexplained Deaths at the Hands of the Secret Government

June 24, 2004: Dr. Assefa Tulu, age 45. Dr. Tulu joined the health department in 1997 and served for five years as the county's lone epidemiologist. He was charged with tracking the health of the county, including the spread of diseases, such as syphilis, AIDS and measles. He also designed a system for detecting a bioterrorism attack involving viruses or bacterial agents. Tulu often coordinated efforts to address major health concerns in Dallas County, such as the West Nile virus outbreaks of the past few years, and worked with the media to inform the public. The Dallas County's chief epidemiologist, was found dead at his desk, allegedly died of a stroke.

June 27, 2004: Dr. Paul Norman, Of Salisbury, Wiltshire, age 52. Norman was the chief scientist for chemical and biological defense at the Ministry of Defence's laboratory at Porton Down, Wiltshire. He traveled the world lecturing on the subject of weapons of mass destruction. Norman was killed when a Cessna 206 he was in crashed shortly after taking off from Dunkeswell Airfield on Sunday. A father and daughter also died at the scene, and 44-year-old parachute instructor and Royal Marine Major Mike Wills later died in the hospital.

John Mullen, of Chesterfield, Missouri, a nuclear physicist and former McDonnell Douglas Corp. research scientist who died suddenly on June 29 2004, was deliberately killed with a massive dose of arsenic. An investigator in this St. Louis suburb said toxicology tests showed that the 67-year-old scientist died of acute arsenic intoxication within hours of complaining of an upset stomach at his home.

July 21, 2004: Dr. John Badwey, age 54. Badwey was a scientist and accidental politician when he opposed disposal of sewage waste program of exposing humans to sludge. He was a biochemist at Harvard Medical School specializing in infectious diseases. Badwey suddenly developed pneumonia-like symptoms then died two weeks later.

August 12, 2004: Professor John Clark, head of the science lab that created Dolly the sheep, the animal cloned from an adult. Prof Clark led the Roslin Institute in Midlothian, one of the world's leading animal biotechnology research centers. He played a crucial role in creating the transgenic sheep that earned the institute worldwide fame. Clark died of an apparent suicide when he was found hanging by his neck in his holiday home. His co-workers were stunned, stating that Professor Clark had no reason to kill himself.

January 7, 2005: Jeong H. Im, age 72. A retired research assistant professor at the University of Missouri-Columbia who was primarily a protein chemist. Someone stabbed the 72-year-old scientist multiple times in the Maryland Avenue parking garage at the University of Missouri-Columbia, put him in the trunk of his Honda and set the car on fire. Adding to the mystery, police say a hooded, masked man was seen carrying a gas can away from the scene. Police have yet to discover a motive for Im's gruesome murder.

The pattern that is emerging would be disturbing to any statistician. The list of dead scientists is factual, and it appears strange that this is happening to people who are in a certain profession. It cannot be denied that these scientists died under mysterious circumstances. The questions remain; for what reason did they die, and who killed them?

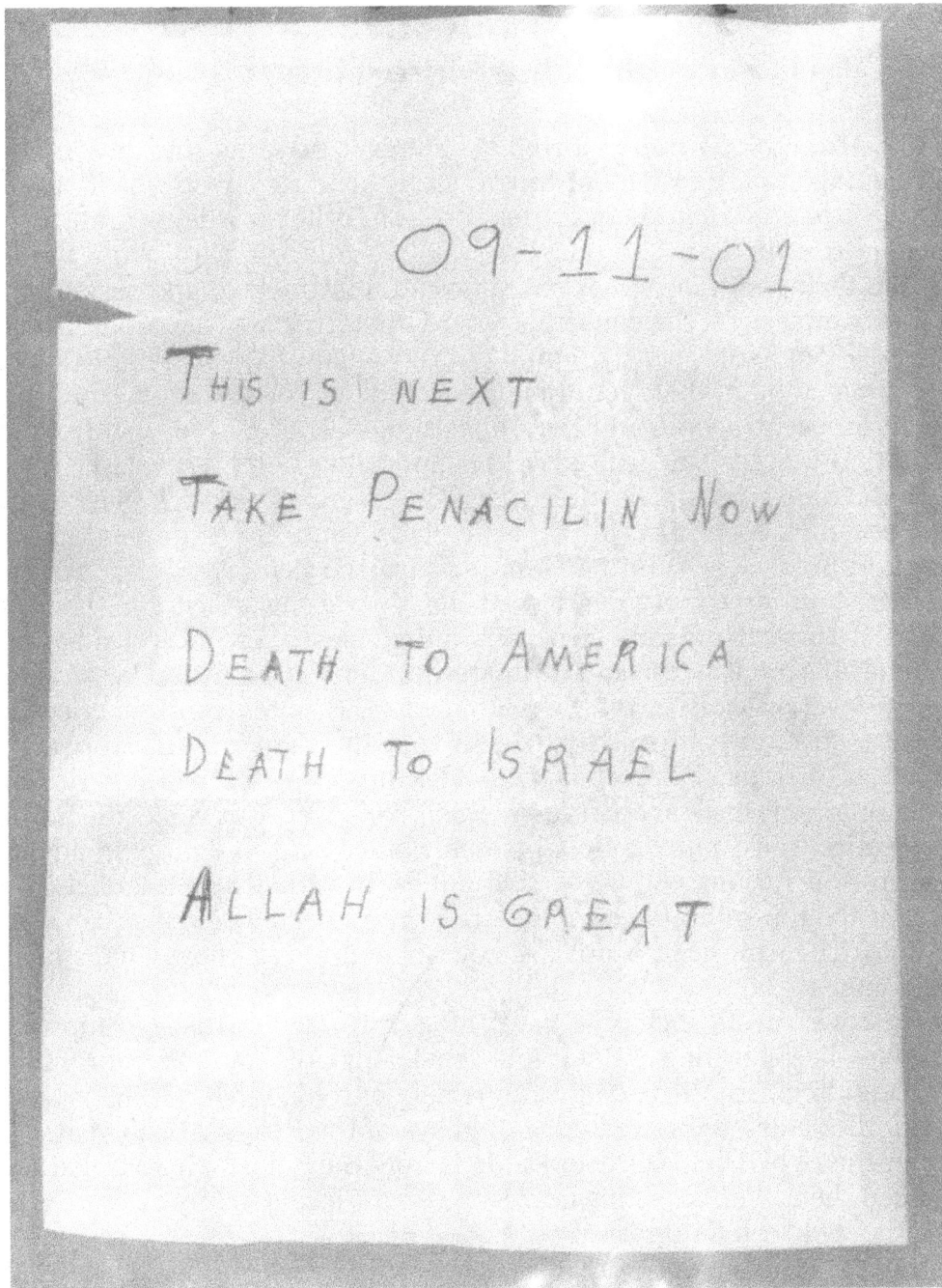

With the anthrax letters coming so soon after the deadly attacks of 9/11, the citizenry of the U.S. were more-than-willing to give up their rights and freedoms in exchange for guarantees of safety from foreign terrorists.

CHAPTER SEVEN
Just One More Thing

The **Moscow Times** reported in January 2005 that they revealed in 2003 a secret Pentagon plan to foment terrorism by sending covert agents to infiltrate terrorist groups and goad them into action – in other words, committing acts of murder and destruction. The purpose was two-fold: first, to bring the terrorist groups into the open, where they could be counterattacked; and second, to justify U.S. military attacks on the countries where the terrorists were operating, attacks which, in the Pentagon's words, would put those nations "sovereignty at risk."

It was a plan that countenanced, indeed, encouraged, the deliberate murder of innocent people and the imposition of U.S. military rule anywhere in the world that U.S. leaders desired. This plan is now being activated.

In fact, it's being expanded, as the **New Yorker's** Seymour Hersh revealed recently. Not only will U.S.-directed agents infiltrate existing terrorist groups and provoke them into action, but also the Pentagon itself will create its own terrorist groups and "death squads." After establishing their terrorist "credentials" through various atrocities and crimes, these American-run groups will then be able to ally with, and ultimately undermine, existing terrorist groups.

Top-level officials in the Pentagon, the U.S. intelligence services and the Bush administration confirmed to Hersh that the plan is going forward, under the direction of Defense Secretary Donald Rumsfeld. Through a series of secret executive orders, President George W. Bush has given Rumsfeld the authority to turn the entire world into "a global free-fire zone," a top Pentagon adviser says. These secret operations will be carried out with virtually no oversight; in many cases, even the top military commanders in the affected regions will not be told about them. The American people, of course, will never know what's being done in their name.

The covert units, including the Pentagon-funded terrorist groups and hit Squads, will be operating outside all constraints of law and morality. "We're going to be riding with the bad boys," one insider told Hersh.

Another likened it to the good old days of the Reagan-Bush years: "Do you remember the right-wing execution squads in El Salvador? We founded them and we financed them. The objective now is to recruit locals in any area we want. And we aren't going to tell Congress about it."

Indeed, Bush has already budgeted $500 million to fund local paramilitaries and guerrilla groups in the most volatile areas of the world, a measure guaranteed to produce needless bloodshed, destruction and suffering for innocent people already ravaged by conflict. The activation of the Pentagon terrorist operation is part of Bush's second-term expansion of the "war on terror."

Despite some obfuscating rhetoric about diplomacy, the Bush regime is pressing ahead with a hard-line strategy aimed at opening new military fronts in the global free-fire zone. Any dissenting voices within the government are being ruthlessly purged. The Pentagon's secret forces are set for operations in at least 10 countries, and Bush insiders "repeatedly" told Hersh that Iran is the next strategic target.

Woman Who Claimed President Bush Raped Her, Found Dead

A Texas woman who claimed to have been raped by President George W. Bush, and was planning to take him to court, died of a mysterious gun shot wound to the head. The Harris County, Texas Examiner's Office, officially registered the 2003 death of Margie Schoedinger, 38, as a suicide.

Schoedinger of Sugar Land, Texas, had filed a lawsuit against President Bush (a former Governor of Texas) in December 2002 accusing him of a series of 'individual sex crimes' against her and her husband. In the seven-page document, filed at Fort Bend County Court in Texas, Schoedinger claimed that Bush had abducted, drugged, raped and beat her. She also suggested that she 'dated George W Bush as a minor', and the President may have been the father of a child she miscarried following the alleged rape.

Schoedinger said she had filed the lawsuit on December 3, 2002 and although court documents filed on the following day mention Bush and offer him 20 days to respond or appear in Fort Bend, it is still unclear whether the President was ever served with the suit. Schoedinger was attempting to claim $1 million in actual damages, plus $49 million for punitive damages including emotional distress and loss of freedom.

When she spoke to journalist Jackson Thoreau, Schoedinger said that the President had personally contacted her to say that he wanted her dead, but could trust no one to carry out the crime. Of the lawsuit she said: "I am still trying to prosecute, but as yet, I haven't had a court date set. I want to get this matter settled and go on with my life. People have to be accountable for what they do and that is why I am pursuing this lawsuit."

The U.S. media had largely ignored the filing of the lawsuit and the story had only appeared in a local newspaper. Her subsequent suicide has raised many eyebrows amongst those who learned of her death via the Internet. Even though the sequence of events was bizarre, again the American media ignored Schoedinger completely.

However, the U.S. press was not alone with the story's media blackout. Both the **London Times** newspaper and the BBC as well as other major news organizations in the UK were furnished with the story and sources for the original court filings. This should have garnered some attention for the story from the big media sources, if only to ridicule the allegations. Instead, in the same way the American media served its audience a stream of controlled news, so too did the British media by pretending Schoedinger didn't exist.

Schoedinger apparently committed suicide on September 22 of 2003, but her death only attracted new attention on the Internet in November of 2003. Only recently has one small-circulation newspaper in the UK (the **New Nation**) run the story of her demise. It found the story so newsworthy it ran its headline on the front page next to the title header.

Many regular readers of "quality" newspapers and TV news have never heard of Margie Schoedinger. Her tale illustrates how the news available on the Internet is often of greater value than that which is paid for. Those who read the papers and watch the news need to ask why this story has been covered up.

Suffer Little Children

Another earth-shaking story that has been largely ignored by the media is the training of children through sexual abuse and mind control to become "sleeper" assassins and terrorists. Documents discovered through Freedom of Information searches show that top-secret programs, such as the CIA's MK-ULTRA operation, were actively researching the possibilities of creating a real "Manchurian Candidate" who could be programmed to kill on command, yet remember nothing afterwards.

The chairman of the Department of Psychology at Colgate University, Dr. Estabrooks, has stated, "I can hypnotize a man without his knowledge or consent into committing treason against the United States."

Estabrooks was one of the nation's most authoritative sources in the hypnotic field. The psychologist told officials in Washington that a mere 200 well-trained hypnotists could develop an army of mind-controlled sixth columnists in wartime United States. He laid out a scenario of an enemy doctor placing thousands of patients under hypnotic mind control, and eventually programming key military officers to follow his assignment. Through such maneuvers, he said, the entire U.S. Army could be taken over. Large numbers of saboteurs could also be created using hypnotism through the work of a doctor practicing in a neighborhood or foreign-born nationals with close cultural ties with an enemy power.

Dr. Estabrooks actually conducted experiments on U.S. soldiers to prove his point. Soldiers of low rank and little formal education were placed under hypnotism and their memories tested. Surprisingly, hypnotists were able to control the subjects' ability to retain complicated verbal information.

J. G. Watkins followed in Estabrooks steps and induced soldiers of lower rank to commit acts that conflicted not only with their moral code, but also the military code that they had come to accept through their basic training. One of the experiments involved placing a normal, stable army private in a deep trance. Watkins was trying to see if he could get the private to attack a superior officer, a cardinal sin in the military.

While the private was in a deep trance, Watkins told him that the officer sitting across from him was an enemy soldier who was going to attempt to kill him. In the private's mind, it was a kill-or-be-killed situation. The private immediately jumped up and grabbed the officer by the throat. The experiment was repeated several times, and in one case the man who was hypnotized and the man who was attacked were very close friends. The results were always the same. In one experiment, the hypnotized subject pulled out a knife and nearly stabbed another person.

One program that has come to light is Project Monarch, a U.S. Defense Department project that was started in the 1960's. It has been alleged that Monarch sought to create junior assassins with multiple personalities, each trained to perform a specific specialty. The kids were programmed to respond to codes, mnemonic cues, and audio-reversed triggers and tones. They were trained in killing techniques and the rapid assembly and de-assembly of exotic weapons.

They were educated about poisons, explosives, languages and computers, then programmed to forget it all or remember only selected areas upon command.

Monarch produced a group of child spies who were directed to prey upon high placed military, government and high society pedophiles, sometimes hauling them into blackmail situations. There is evidence of selected breeding, adoption of the children, and a peculiarly large number of twins among the group.

A number of so-called religious cults and fundamental Christian churches are believed to actually be fronts for the training of mind controlled soldiers and terrorists. The Branch Davidians in Waco, Texas and Jim Jones Peoples Temple were both intelligence operations with the purpose of recruiting families so that their children could be trained for later service.

One group that has so far managed to escape public notice is The Finders, an obscure group based in Washington DC. The Finders originated in the early 1970s (known as The Seekers in those days) under the direction of Marion Pettie. Pettie is believed to be a CIA agent whose mission was to create a religious "group" for mind control training. As with other groups, special emphasis was given to find children, as their minds are much easier to condition.

The Finders would have continued to operate completely unseen if it had not been for a police investigation in 1987 when two men, Michael Houlihan and Douglas Ammerman, who were traveling with six children, were arrested in a Tallahassee, Florida park. The children, identified in a court document only by the first names of Honeybee, John, Franklin, Bee Bee, Max and Mary, were described as "dirty, unkempt, hungry, disturbed and agitated."

The children, along with the two men, had been living in the rear of a van for some time. One of the children, a 6 yr. old girl, showed signs of sexual abuse. Five of the children were uncommunicative, according to police, and none seemed to recognize objects such as typewriters and staplers. However, the oldest was able to give investigators some information. She said that the two men "were their teachers."

Before their arrests in the park, the two adult caretakers had told police that they were teachers from Washington DC "transporting these children to Mexico and a school for brilliant children." When police asked the men where the children's mothers were they said they were being weaned from their mothers.

Washington DC police, who searched a Northeast Washington warehouse linked to the group, removed large plastic bags filled with color slides, photographs and photographic contact sheets. Some photos visible through a bag carried from the warehouse were wallet-sized pictures of children, similar to school photos, and some were of naked children. DC police sources said some of the items seized were detailed instructions on obtaining children for unknown purposes and pictures of children engaged in what appeared to be "cult rituals."

Officials of the U.S. Customs Service, called in to aid in the investigation, said that the material seized included photos showing children involved in sexual situations, bloodletting ceremonies of animals, and one photograph of a child in chains. Customs officials looked into whether a child pornography operation was being conducted. However, due to the intervention from what one official described as "someone very far up the chain of command in the government," all charges and investigations against The Finders were halted.

It is clear that The Finders are somehow linked to the CIA. Customs Service documents reveal that in 1987, when Customs agents sought to examine the evidence gathered by Washington, DC police, they were told that The Finders investigation "had become an internal matter."

The police report on the case had been classified secret. Even now, Tallahassee police complain about the handling of The Finders investigation by DC police.

"They dropped this case," one Tallahassee investigator says, "like a hot rock."

DC police refuse to comment on the matter. As for the CIA, ranking officials describe allegations about links between the intelligence agency and the Finders as 'hogwash,' perhaps the result of a simple mix up with DC police. The only connection, according to the CIA is a firm that provided computer training to CIA officers also employed several members of The Finders.

It should probably be noted that the firm that supplied the training to CIA officers did not just employ several members of The Finders, but appears to have in fact been a wholly owned subsidiary of The Finders organization. It should also be noted that the CIA does not, as a general rule-of-thumb, assign the training of its officers to outside contractors, so the firm must be a CIA front.

The CIA's interest in the Finders may stem from the fact that group leader Pettie's late wife once worked for the agency and that his son worked for a CIA proprietary firm, Air America.

When custom officials raided the Washington DC buildings used by The Finders, they found several computers, printers, and numerous documents. Cursory examination of the documents revealed detailed instructions for obtaining children for unspecified purposes.

The instructions included the impregnation of female members of The Finders, purchasing children, trading, and kidnapping. There were telex messages using MCI account numbers between a computer terminal believed to be located in the same room, and others located across the country and in foreign locations.

One such telex specifically ordered the purchase of two children in Hong Kong to be arranged through a contact in the Chinese Embassy there. Another telex expressed interest in "bank secrecy" situations. Other documents identified interests in high-tech transfers to the United Kingdom, numerous properties under the control of The Finders, a keen interest in terrorism, explosives, and the evasion of law enforcement.

Also found in the computer room was a detailed summary of the events surrounding the arrest and taking into custody of the two adults and six children in Tallahassee. There was also a set of instructions that appeared to be broadcast via a computer network that advised the participants to move "the children" and keep them moving through different jurisdictions, and instructions on how to avoid police attention. As well, there was a large collection of photographs of unidentified persons discovered. Some of the photographs were nudes, believed to be of members of The Finders. Numerous photos of nude children were also found. At least one of which was a photo of a child on display and appearing to accent the child's genitals.

Further inspection of the premises disclosed numerous files relating to activities of the organization in different parts of the world. Locations observed are as follows: London, Germany, the Bahamas, Japan, Hong Kong, Malaysia, Africa, Costa Rica, and Europe. There was also a file identified as Palestinian.

Other files were identified by member name or 'project' name, with the projects appearing to be operated for commercial purposes under front names for The Finders. There was one file entitled "Pentagon Break-In," and others referring to members operating in foreign countries.

There were also intelligence files on private families not related to The Finders. The process undertaken appears to be have been a systematic response to local newspaper advertisements for babysitters, tutors, etc. A member of The Finders would respond and gather as much information as possible about the habits, identity, occupation, etc., of the family. The use to which this information was to be put is still unknown.

There was also a large amount of data collected on various childcare organizations. The warehouse contained a large library, two kitchens, a sauna, hot tub, and a video room. The video room seemed to be set up as an indoctrination center. It also appeared that the organization had the capability to produce its own videos.

There were what appeared to be training areas for children and what appeared to be an altar set up in a residential area of the warehouse. Many jars of urine and feces were located in this area.

When Tallahassee detectives tried to pursue the case against the finders, Washington DC police told them all passport data from The Finders had been turned over to the State Department for their investigation. The State Department, in turn, said that all travel and use of the passports by the holders of the passports was within the law and no action would be taken. This included travel to Moscow, North Korea, and North Vietnam from the late 1950s to mid 1970s.

Tallahassee police were also told that the investigation into the activity of The Finders had become a CIA internal matter. The police report had been classified SECRET and was not available for review. As well, the FBI had withdrawn from the investigation several weeks prior and that the FBI Foreign Counter Intelligence Division had directed the police not to advise the FBI Washington Field Office of anything that had transpired.

Independent investigators have uncovered good evidence that groups like The Finders and now even evangelical Christian churches associated with prominent TV evangelists, are actually intelligence operations of the CIA. These religious organizations use tried and true mind control techniques on their congregations to create a new citizenry who believes that God sanctions everything the U.S. government does. Even more frightening, children in these groups are sought out for extensive mind control training that includes sexual molestation and rape by adults.

Strange and Unexplained Deaths at the Hands of the Secret Government

Researcher Arlene Tyner, who has spent a considerable amount of time interviewing and corresponding with victims of mind control operations, noted in a **Probe** magazine article that many of these victims "were turned over to military/CIA doctors by pedophile fathers or other sexually abusive relatives. CIA officials also blackmailed family members known to produce child porn in order to gain control of their already abused and psychologically fragmented children."

It is certainly within the realm of possibility that the high profile child pornography raids in recent years, which invariably result in relatively few arrests and even fewer prosecutions and convictions, are not intended to punish the victimizers, but to identify and compromise them. It not inconceivable that the databases being compiled will be utilized as something of a recruitment list to identify those persons who have been "preconditioned," so to speak, for future mind control operations.

Nazi scientists during WWII discovered that children, who were repeatedly raped and exposed to graphic sexual imagery, would often mentally disassociate and create alternate personalities in order to cope with the physical and mental torture. Many of these Nazi scientists were brought to the United States at the end of the war and allowed to continue their research for the military and intelligence services.

It was then fairly simple to train one of these multiple personalities in the art of warfare and assassination. A person could live their entire life not realizing that they had multiple personalities that could be "turned on" with a simple phrase or visual image and instructed to perform an assigned task.

The final stage of programming usually occurs on military bases to insure security. Two bases that have been exposed in the past by incidents are Offutt and the Presidio in the 1980s. The Presidio case dates back as far as 1982, when a military doctor warned the army of the danger to children in its day care center. The army failed to follow its own regulations in allowing the children to go on field trips off base without the parents consent. On August 14, 1984, the FBI and officers from the army's criminal investigation division raided the home of Lt. Col. Michael Aquino looking for evidence of child molestation.

The evidence against Col. Aquino was overwhelming, but to the dismay of the victim's parents, all charges were dropped. Col. Aquino has reportedly developed training tapes on how to create a mind control slave and worked as a liaison between government/military intelligence and various criminal organizations in the distribution of mind control slaves.

The Presidio case attracted the attention of investigative reporter and radio talk show host, Mae Bruessell. During her investigation of the case, she received several death threats and her daughter was killed in a car wreck that Bruessell attributed as a hit. Before concluding her investigation, Mae was struck with a fast onset of cancer. It is suspected that Bruessell's death may have been induced rather than from natural causes.

Many of the children subjected to the mind control techniques, according to New Orleans psychologist Valerie Wolf, were fragmented by trauma-based programming into a spate of alternate personalities: "Most of these patients responded to certain sounds," Wolf reported in testimony to the President's

Advisory Committee on Radiation Experiments on March 15, 1995, "clickers, metronomes or just clicking the tongue or hand clapping. Patients would vacillate from calm to robotically asking, 'Who do you want me to kill?'"

It was also revealed that post-hypnotic commands had been implanted in subjects just in case therapists ever attempted to delve to deeply into their patient's psyche. They were then triggered to attempt suicide and attack the therapist, or march out of the office in a fugue state to assassinate somebody.

Claudia Mullens, a survivor of the experiments, testified at the Advisory Committee hearings about a trip in 1959 to the Deer Creek camp in Maryland, then used to train child prostitutes for sexual blackmail operations. At the camp, she was the "guest" of a Mr. Sheiber, an alias of the CIA's notorious mind control researcher, Dr. Sidney Gottleib:

"Most of the men I came to know well were either there as observers or volunteer targets. We were taught different ways to please men and at the same time ask questions to get them to talk about themselves. Then we had to recall everything about them. After this trip, I mainly went to hospitals, Army or Air Force bases or universities or the hotels in New Orleans and a place called the TRIMS facility in Texas."

"Most patients," Wolf testified at the Advisory Committee hearings, "reported neo-Nazi alter personalities who believed in the coming of the next Reich."

Other symptoms of survivors include grand mal epileptic seizures with a temporary cessation of breathing. Doctors managed to strap one survivor to an EEG machine in the midst of a seizure — his brain waves registered normal. The fit was not a true grand mal, but a body memory of electric shocks.

"Electroshock was often used on various parts of the body," Wolf said, "usually the physical places that do not readily show or in tissue that heals quickly." High technology has been combined with drugs, hypnosis and torture to create alter personalities. Years before computers and virtual-reality, some children reportedly told psychotherapists they'd been forced to wear goggles that flashed 3-D images of horror and death.

Since a number of people who were brainwashed, tortured and drugged in these experiments try to resolve their experiences in therapy, psychiatrists and other professional therapists are hearing these stories. They are told, for example, that CIA controllers sometimes dressed up in satanic costumes to further traumatize the children, also providing a cover that wouldn't be believed if the children ever talked.

Many of the strange deaths that have been covered in this book have no doubt been carried out by mind control assassins who have been trained through various techniques to carry out their grim duty with no remorse and no memory of their actions. As well, many of these unfortunate souls have been, and are now being readied to carry out covert terrorist strikes not only in targeted foreign countries, but also in the United States.

We have already seen cases of domestic terrorism such as the bombing of abortion clinics, Planned Parenthood, and the assassinations of certain politicians. There could also be a connection between mind control assassins and the shooting rampages that have overtaken many schools. It could be that the students involved are mind control victims that have either been deliberately triggered to kill, or who's programming was accidentally initiated at the wrong time.

The United States government is increasingly using the threat of terrorism to keep the population frightened and pliable. During the election of 2004, President George W. Bush and Vice President Dick Cheney constantly reminded voters that if they should vote for the Democratic candidate, terrorists would attack the U.S. with biological and nuclear weapons. It was obvious that these were thinly veiled threats: "If you vote for the other guy, you will die."

In the early 1960's the Pentagon came up with its own form of domestic terrorism called "Operation Northwoods." In response to the Bay-of-Pigs failure in Cuba, the Joint Chiefs of Staff in 1962 came up with a plan to covertly engineer various terrorist operations within the United States that would justify a U.S. invasion of Cuba.

These proposals – part of a secret anti-Castro program known as Operation Mongoose – included staging the assassinations of Cubans living in the United States, developing a fake "Communist Cuban terror campaign in the Miami area, in other Florida cities and even in Washington," including "sinking a boatload of Cuban refugees (real or simulated)," faking a Cuban air force attack on a civilian jetliner, and concocting a "Remember the Maine" incident by blowing up a U.S. ship in Cuban waters and then blaming the incident on Cuban sabotage.

Knowing what we know now about Operation Northwoods, mind control assassins and terrorists, it is extremely probable that recent terrorist attacks, such as what occurred on 9/11, were instigated by secret agencies within the U.S. government with the purpose of expanding the military influence of the United States worldwide.

Those who have stood in the way, now and in the past, have been silenced forever. We should look carefully at every death that strikes those in the public eye who have stood up against the tyranny that is spreading across this land. It is essential that their voices are not silenced and that the things that we all hold so dear, our rights and freedoms, should not be given away under the pretense of protection from terrorism.

• • •

For more information about this and other conspiracies, write for our free Conspiracy Journal Catalog:

Global Communications
P.O. Box 753
New Brunswick, NJ 08903

Visit our website: www.conspiracyjournal.com

CONTINUED ON NEXT PAGE >

134

www.ingramcontent.com/pod-product-compliance
Lightning Source LLC
Chambersburg PA
CBHW080050280326
41934CB00014B/3275